'AUGUSTINIANISM'

STUDIES IN SPIRITUALITY SUPPLEMENTS
Edited by Titus Brandsma Institute – Nijmegen – The Netherlands

2. Franco Imoda, *Human Development. Psychology and Mystery*, 1998, 397 p., ISBN: 90-429-0028-8.

3. Marieke van Baest, *Poetry of Hadewijch*, 1998, VIII-330 p., ISBN: 90-429-0668-7.

4. Hildegard Elisabeth Keller, *My Secret is Mine. Studies on Religion and Eros in the German Middle Ages*, 2000, VIII-294 p., ISBN: 90-429-0871-8.

5. Franco Imoda, *A Journey to Freedom. An Interdisciplinary Approach to the Anthropology of Formation*, 2000, XIV-482 p., ISBN: 90-429-0894-7.

6. Albrecht Classen, *'Mein Seel fang an zu singen'. Religiöse Frauenlieder des 15.-16. Jahrhunderts. Kritische Studien und Textedition*, 2002, 395 p., ISBN: 90-429-1098-4.

7. Marie L. Baird, *On the Side of the Angels. Ethics and Post-Holocaust Spirituality*, 2002, 143 p., ISBN: 90-429-1156-5.

8. Kees Waaijman, *Spirituality. Forms, Foundations, Methods*, 2002, VIII-968 p., ISBN: 90-429-1183-2.

9. John D. Green, *'A Strange Tongue'. Tradition, Language and the Appropriation of Mystical Experiences in the Late Fourteenth-Century England and Sixteenth-Century Spain*, 2002, VII-227 p., ISBN: 90-429-1236-7.

10. Hein Blommestijn, Charles Caspers and Rijcklof Hofman (Eds.), *Spirituality Renewed. Studies on Significant Representatives of the Modern Devotion*, 2003, VI-276 p., ISBN: 90-429-1327-4.

11. Donald J. Moores, *Mystical Discourse in Wordsworth and Whitman. A Transatlantic Bridge*, 2006, VII-286 p., ISBN: 90-429-1809-8.

12. Alessandro Manenti, Stefano Guarinelli and Hans Zollner (Eds.), *Formation an the Person. Essays on Theory and Practice*, 2007, VIII-303 p., ISBN 978-90-429-1881-8.

13. Elisabeth Hense, *Die Kammer der Andacht. Formbeschreibung einer Theaterproduktion*, 2007, X-114 p., ISBN 978-90-429-1966-2.

STUDIES IN SPIRITUALITY
Supplement 14

'AUGUSTINIANISM'

Studies in the Process of Spiritual Transvaluation

by

J.D. Green

PEETERS
LEUVEN - PARIS - DUDLEY, MA
2007

A CIP record for this book is available from the Library of Congress.

© 2007, Peeters, Bondgenotenlaan 153, B-3000 Leuven

ISBN 978-90-429-1976-1
D. 2007/0602/118

PREFACE

The studies in this book have been published as independent articles in the *Australasian Catholic Record*. However they are about a similar historical problem and share the common themes of 'spiritual transvaluation' and Augustine of Hippo's influence on Christian spirituality in the mediaeval period. The first study is about how Augustine's own thought evolved in a 'transvaluation' process and those which follow, about how aspects of his thought were appropriated by important spiritual masters in a similar process.

The notion of 'spiritual transvaluation' takes its particular meaning from the context in which it is used. The process has two components. The first is movement in space, time, or ethos in the same sense that transmission, translation, and transcendence are notions about a 'crossing over'. The second is judgement in the sense of 'evaluation'. In the context of Augustine's influence the process drives the mediation between continuity and change in the spiritual perception of those who relate their own experience to his teaching.

It seemed appropriate to collect the studies together because together they suggest how 'Augustinianism' evolved, not so much as a consistent body of thought, but as a method of evaluation and as a spiritual ambience which suffused the self-understanding of the masters about their spiritual experience. In the process the individuality of the masters' own teaching was coloured. The cumulative effect was a spiritual focus which might legitimately be called 'Augustinianism' in its spiritual dimension.

This thesis can only be regarded as suggestive. It is drawn from a small sample of spiritual masters living in different times and circumstances within the mediaeval period. Moreover the masters interrogate an expanding contemplative tradition which itself draws on diverse Christian experiences and successive interpretations of Augustine's thought. Nevertheless the attempt to understand the counterpoint between Augustine's experience and self-understanding and the similar counterpoint in the experiences of spiritual masters who follow him seems to provide a fruitful way to investigate the elusive, but real, nature of Augustine's influence without compromising the independence and stature of the contributions to Christian spirituality of the spiritual masters concerned.

For me the production of this book has been the rewarding experience of revisiting, and further exploring, questions which have long puzzled me about the manner in which Augustine's teaching was appropriated in the mediaeval period. I would like to record my gratitude to those who, both in recent and more remote times, made it possible.

Firstly I thank Dr. Hein Blommestijn and the Editorial Board at the Titus Brandsma Instituut for publishing the book and, particularly, Drs. Wendy Litjens who prepared the manuscript for publication. Secondly I thank Rev. Gerard Kelly and the Editorial Board of the *Australasian Catholic Record* for publishing my articles and in particular Rev. Dr. Austin Cooper omi who encouraged me 'to keep writing'. In the past, Professor Greg Dening supervised all my post-graduate work at the University of Melbourne and made it a most rewarding experience. The studies on which the book is based are largely derived from the research undertaken during this period. In the very remote past, the late Rev. Dr. Vivian Green, then Senior Tutor, at Lincoln College, Oxford, first stimulated my interest in mediaeval history by asking the questions which revealed the inadequacy of my reading. He also arranged for me to take tutorials with the late Rev. Dr. T. M. Parker in the 'Augustine' Special Subject. This turned out to be a ground breaking experience for me. As Professor Peter Brown has so eloquently put it the 'Augustine' Special Subject was 'a precarious bridge flung out by the [former Modern History] syllabus between ancient and mediaeval history, between the disciplines of the historian, the theologian and the philosopher.' It fuelled the interest which ultimately led to the writing of this book.

Finally I must thank my wife, Mary, and the family for their encouragement and patience over a long period. In particular I owe a debt of gratitude to Damian and Justin for their generosity with computers and patiently coaching me in computing and word processing to a standard at least adequate to the task, no mean feat I am afraid.

CONTENTS

PREFACE   V

PROLOGUE   1

CHAPTER I   St Augustine of Hippo   5
  The Late Antique Milieu   7
  Augustine's 'Conversion'   11
  The Characteristics of Augustine's 'Christian Philosophy'   12
  The *Confessions*   18
  De Trinitate   23
  Discourses on the Psalms   27
  Reflection   28

CHAPTER II   St Gregory the Great   33
  The Two Lives   35
  Contemplation   38
  The Vision of 'God'   40
  Love   43
  Charity   46
  Reflection   48

CHAPTER III   William of St Thierry   53
  Schola Caritatis   57
  'The Likeness'   63
  'Amor Intellectus Est'   66
  Reflection   68

CHAPTER IV   Walter Hilton   73
  The Two Lives   81
  The Contemplative Process   86
  Knowledge of God   91
  Grace   93
  'The Image and Likeness' theme   94
  Reflection   97

EPILOGUE   101

SELECT BIBLIOGRAPHY   105

PROLOGUE

Tertullian, the Christian convert and theologian, writing at the turn of the third century, had thrown out the challenge to his Gnostic opponents: 'What has Athens to do with Jerusalem?'[1] His answer had been: 'Our instruction comes from "the porch of Solomon"'. His North African compatriot, St Augustine of Hippo, himself a convert but living at the turn of the fifth century, would not have disagreed. Nevertheless Augustine travelled to 'the porch of Solomon' by way of Athens. In doing so he demonstrated how they were related and in the process produced a body of teaching, which was of seminal importance to the understanding of what was meant by Christian faith. He consolidated the achievement by living the faith he preached.

'Augustinianism' defies definition because it is a symbol which continues to accumulate meaning as time passes. It is the creation of numerous individuals who have demonstrated in their lives and teaching how Augustine's 'attitude of love' might be applied to develop some aspect of his thought which was germane to their own circumstances.

This is a study of 'Augustinianism' as a process of transvaluation. It is a description of 'Augustinianism' in this limited way and while by no means comprehensive, it may illustrate, hopefully, the way in which Augustine's influence has been transmitted as a developing tradition of spirituality which is recognisably 'Augustinian' in its seminal inspiration.

The first chapter deals with Augustine's own appropriation of the Christian faith as a transvaluation process. His conversion to Christianity was both a moral and intellectual process. Both aspects were marked by particular events but developed in parallel as his understanding of the reciprocal relevance of the Hellenic 'religio-philosophic' and Judaeo-Christian inheritances became clear in the challenges he faced as a Christian pastor. For Augustine the 'moral' conversion came first and enabled him to develop the Hellenic traditions as the handmaid of the Christian. In doing so he was able to articulate a philosophic structure for the 'faith' dependent on a creator whose love was both boundless and ever-present.

Augustine evolved a method through which faith might be developed and understood. It was not a 'system'. This characteristic gave his teaching the appearance of a resource, like a dictionary or encyclopaedia, which was a guide to the 'language' of faith and a series of articles about it, both of which needed additions and updating as times changed.

---

[1] Tertullian (c160-c225), *De praescriptione haereticum*, 7, 'Quid Athenae hierosolymis?'

Yet his teaching had to be preserved if the resource was to be made available to future generations. That it was preserved and widely disseminated was partly the result of his own foresight and brilliance and partly that of the development of monastic styles of Christian community.

Augustine's *Retractions* illustrates his foresight.[2] In the last years of his life he edited the vast volume of his works which had been carefully stored in his library and where necessary revised them. The process of revision which he undertook in the light of the development of his thought illustrates how new circumstances change the teacher's perspective and suggests that 'transvaluation' is not a process of unimaginative imitation but is based on the counterpoint between faith and experience.

The monastic community he formed around him as bishop of Hippo, produced 'disciples' familiar with his library if not fully able to grasp its import. One of his 'disciples', Possidius, bishop of Calama, in the last days of Augustine's life when Hippo was under siege, catalogued the library. How, after the siege, it was transported to Rome is still a puzzle. Nevertheless, the service Possidius rendered in cataloguing the library assisted the process of preservation.[3]

The development of monasticism as a combination of prayer, reflection and study, was a key factor both in the preservation and dissemination of Augustine's works.

It is no accident that when one looks for exemplars of 'Augustinianism', they are found in monastic communities or in people with monastic connections. This study is structured around three case studies. The masters whose teaching is explored in all of them have monastic connections and indeed lived in times when the monastic life was at a critical period of its evolution.

The first of these is St Gregory the Great at the turn of the seventh century. In many respects his spiritual evolution paralleled that of Augustine. His great achievements were reflected in the honour bestowed on him by the Church as 'the Great'. His contemplative experience as a founder of monasteries and as an abbot enabled him to appropriate Augustine's spirituality as his own. His great prestige in the following centuries gave authority to his teaching and, to the extent that he absorbed it, to Augustine's teaching also. Gregory thus became an important channel through whose works Augustine's influence was disseminated.

The subject of the second case study is William of St Thierry in the twelfth century. William was both the abbot of a Benedictine monastery of St Thierry near Reims in France and also, later in life, a Cistercian in the new foundation of Signy in the Ardennes. He was primarily a contemplative and a teacher who

---

2   Serge Lancel, *St Augustine*, London: SCM Press, 2002, 458-461.
3   *Ibid.*, 475, 476.

sought to explain his own experience of contemplation to those in his community. His own understanding was based on Augustine's thought but developed
in the light of his own experience. He was also the friend of St Bernard and came
in contact with the Cistercian reform as it developed in the teaching of its most
charismatic advocate. William's most influential work on contemplation, the
Golden Epistle, was for many centuries attributed to St Bernard.[4] Although its
influence reflected its own merits, there is little doubt that its dissemination and
influence owed much to its attribution to St Bernard. To the extent that Augustine's basic insights permeated William's teaching, it also influenced Cistercian
thought in a transvalued form.

The third case study is about Walter Hilton in late fourteenth century England. In the last years of his life he was an Augustinian canon regular living in
a community which practised a form of religious life, partly contemplative and
partly active: The rule combined the monastic tradition of a stable community
with the active evangelical work associated with-the tradition of the mendicant
orders. The fourteenth century was a time of transition in many respects. The
Church authorities were attempting to revive religious practice in the face of
social and political change, the dislocations caused by plague epidemics, and the
heterodox teaching of Wycliffe and the Lollard movement. Hilton's teaching
reflected his experience of spiritual direction for both religious and laity. He had
absorbed Augustine's teaching and transvalued it to meet the pedagogical challenges he faced. The number of extant manuscripts of his major work, the *Scale
of Perfection*, suggests a wide dissemination of his teaching and a demand that
perhaps reflects the unsettled nature of the society in which he lived.

These case studies illustrate the way in which Augustine's insights were
appropriated and transvalued in the light of different challenges and an evolv-
ing Christian self-understanding. The Epilogue will attempt to draw together
the main strands of the evolution of 'Augustinianism' as revealed in these studies as counterpoint to Augustine's own experience of the Christian faith and its
appropriation.

---

4   J.M. Déchanet on the history of the *Golden Epistle* in the introduction to *The golden epistle*,
     Kalamazoo: Cistercian Publications, 1971, ixff.

CHAPTER I

ST AUGUSTINE OF HIPPO

The Philosophic Transvaluation of Judaeo-Christian 'Affectivity'

Possidius of Calama begins the preface of his biography of St Augustine with the prophetic words:

> My Subject is the life and character of that best of bishops, Augustine, a man predestined from eternity to be given to us when his time came.[1]

For forty of the seventy-six years of Augustine's life, Possidius had witnessed and participated in the evolution of a great body of teaching as one of the most powerful and curious minds of the Latin Church grappled with the whole range of problems which a rapidly changing society generated.[2] That a mind of Augustine's calibre was on hand at that time was for Possidius 'providential';[3] he sensed intuitively the importance for posterity of the achievement without, perhaps, fully understanding its extent.[4]

Possidius, and others who followed him, transvalued Augustine's work for their constituencies in relation to the context of their experience and to their perceived personal missions. Augustine himself had a similar transvaluation mission. In his case it was related to the Christian inheritance with which he became progressively more familiar after his Baptism. As a priest and bishop his ministry

---

[1] *The life of St Augustine of Hippo* by St Possidius, Bishop of Calama, in the *Western fathers*, (trans. and ed. by F.R. Hoare) London: Sheed and Ward, 1954, 243. The translation is from the *Sancti Augustini scripta a possidio episcopo*, (edited with a revised text, introduction, notes and an English version by Herbert T. Weiskotten) Princeton: Princeton University Press, 1919.

[2] *Ibid.*, 191. Possidius entered St Augustine's community at Hippo about the time of the latter's ordination to the priesthood in 391.

[3] Henry Chadwick, *Augustine*, Oxford: Oxford University Press, 1986, 109. It is interesting to note that Augustine was also a great believer in 'providence'. Chadwick remarks on Augustine's lifelong concern to 'vindicate providence'.

[4] Hoare, *The Western fathers*, 191. With reference to Possidius: 'Nor were his education and culture sufficient to enable him to give any real picture of Augustine's intellectual stature and achievements or to visualise the nature of his future influence'. Both points are literally correct but hardly fair comment.

and mission expanded, as did his constituency. Prior to his Baptism he had achieved a considerable standing in public and academic circles. That standing ensured his constituency would expand beyond the Hippo diocese, to embrace not only the North African littoral but the whole Roman world around the Mediterranean basin. He became engaged in most of the religious controversies of his time, and there were many of them. He was increasingly consulted about interpreting Christian teaching to a whole range of individuals as his vast correspondence testifies. In his major works he established a philosophic framework and a methodology which related Christianity to the intellectual conceptual horizons of Late Antiquity. His achievements in this field will be the main concern of this chapter.

The Judaeo-Christian inheritance is itself a vast and complex subject. It is testimony to the power of Augustine's intellect that he mastered it in a very short space of time. This study will be confined to one aspect of that inheritance, its 'affectivity', by which is meant the nature of the loving relationship between the divine creator and his creation. Augustine appropriated it to a remarkable degree and it 'warmed' in a special way his intellectual efforts to make Christianity intelligible to a constituency that did not think of a divinity both interested in and, caring for, human life. The appropriation also ensured that his work would be relevant to the human condition in all ages, as people confront the 'restlessness' which Augustine diagnosed so acutely in his own condition. Moreover his mastery of the written, as well as the spoken, word enabled him to communicate his own feelings about his subject with added cogency. The cogency was reinforced by the obvious sincerity of the witness of his ministry.

Even by restricting the discussion within these parameters it will inevitably be selective. Furthermore the scholarship associated with Augustinian studies is so vast, and growing, that only a small part has been consulted. However, there are some authorities on Augustine and his period that make the task a little more manageable. The degree to which the discussion is dependent on them will become obvious.

The focus of the study is the nexus between Augustine's discovery of the Hellenic philosophical inheritance and his appropriation of Christian teaching which transvalued both. We will begin with some relevant observations about the Late Antique society in which Augustine lived. The particular aspect of Late Antique culture we wish to highlight is the nexus between philosophy and religion. This discussion will lead into a consideration of Augustine's conversion as the key to his appropriation of the Christian idea of a loving God within a philosophic frame of reference. We will then discuss the emergence of 'Augustinianism' as a formative expression of Christian philosophy. Finally we wish to discuss how the affective/philosophic/mystical ambiance of 'Augustinianism' was mediated by some of the most influential works in which his teaching has been preserved. The particular works we wish to discuss are the *Confessions*,[5] the *De Trinitate*[6] and the *Discourses on the Psalms*[7].

The Late Antique Milieu

The attempt to understand the interaction between Augustine and his cultural milieu can only be cursory in the compass of the present study and will be dependent on the great and growing body of scholarship which has developed about Augustine.[8] Even such a cursory study is necessary not only to understand the interaction between Augustine's teaching and its genesis but also to understand why and how his teaching and methods of analysis became the source of future transvaluations.

The secret of the cogency of St Augustine's teaching may, in part, lie in the range and quality of the stimuli to which he was exposed, the challenges he had to face. Augustine's encounters with Manichees,[9] Donatists,[10] and

---

5 There are a number of translations of the *Confessions*. F.J. Sheed's, (London: Hodder and Stoughton, 1944), has been used in the text; in the notes three sets of numbers are shown; thus X, 31,43 means book X, chapter 31, paragraph 43. The Latin edition used is that of M. Skutella, revised by H. Juergens and W. Schaub, in *Bibliotheca Teubneriana* (Stuttgart: 1969). See also Maria Boulding's translation (London: Hodder and Stoughton, 1999), particularly the introduction.

6 There is an English translation of books VIII-X, XIV and XV by John Burnaby in *Augustine: later works* (Library of Christian Classics, London: SCM Press,1955), which have been used where available. In the notes, book and chapter numbers have been indicated. The Latin edition is *Bibliothèque Augustinienne*, vols. 15 and 16, Paris, 1955.

7 *Enarrationes in Psalmos*. The English title in the translation used is *Expositions on the Book of Psalms*, ed. P. Schaff (from the six volumes of the Oxford translation by A. Cleveland Coxe D.D.), Nicene and Post-Nicene Fathers, Series 1, Vol. VIII, Edinburgh: T. & T. Clark, 1888. In the notes Psalm number and chapter have been cited from this edition. The more familiar title, *Discourses on the Psalms*, has been retained in the text.

8 Peter Brown, *Augustine of Hippo*, London: Faber and Faber, 1967, 10: 'The study of Augustine is endless – though fortunately well-signposted by modern bibliographical collections'. See also 10, n.1: 'Every year, *Le Revue des études augustiniennes* produces an exhaustive "Bulletin" of some 400 titles'.

9 The Manichaean cosmology tended to absolve the individual from personal responsibility for sin. See Brown, *Augustine of Hippo*, 176: 'The avoidance of "confession" now struck Augustine as the hallmark of his Manichaean phase: "it had pleased my pride to be free from a sense of guilt, and when I had done anything wrong not to confess that it was myself who had done it, that You might heal my Soul" (Conf. V,10,18; cf. IV,3,4.)'.

10 See Chadwick, *Augustine*, 81: 'select quotations from Augustine's anti-Donatist writings enabled some mediaeval canonists to make him look as if he were justifying the stern measures against heretics adopted in the later middle ages'. More importantly: 'The grace of God did not depend for its efficacy on the personal sanctity of the individual Minister, but on whether he did what God commanded to be done and thereby showed himself aware that in his sacramental action

Pelagians,[11] perhaps less obviously so, with the pagans of various persuasions such as Academicians[12] and Neoplatonists,[13] represented the range of the intellectual challenges which the Christian Church was to face frequently during succeeding centuries; challenges not necessarily of unbelief but of a questionably based spirituality and morality. The explanation of why these sects grew in strength about this time is one of the central puzzles of Late Antique society:

> The central problem of late Roman religious history is to explain why men came to act out their inner life through suddenly coagulating into new groups, and why they need to find a new focus in the solidarities and sharp boundaries of the sect, the Monastery, the orthodox Empire. The sudden flooding of the inner life into social forms; this is what distinguishes the Late Antique period, of the third century onwards, from the classical world.[14]

Brown rejects the hypothesis that there was a perceptible disintegration of the fabric of society:

> Seldom has any period of European history littered the future with so many irremovable institutions. The codes of Roman Law, the hierarchy of the Catholic Church, the idea of the Christian Empire, the Monastery – up to the eighteenth century, men (...) still turned to those imposing legacies of the institution-building of the Late Antique period for guidance as to how to organise their life in this world.[15]

---

the whole Church is acting'. The Donatist controversy was an important catalyst in the evolution of Augustine's teaching on the 'Church' and the sacraments.

[11] See Brown, *Augustine of Hippo*, 177. Book Ten of the *Confessions* 'deeply annoyed' Pelagius by its tone: '...so that my mind, questioning itself upon its own powers, feels it cannot rightly trust its own report' (Conf., X, 32, 48). 'The Pelagian was *emancipatus a deo* (*Op. Imp.* 1,78)' (Brown, 352). The individual had the capacity to attain perfection without God's help. The opposing views on human nature are the crux of the difference between Pelagius and Augustine. But as Brown aptly observes: 'Indeed Pelagianism, as we know it, that consistent body of ideas of momentous consequences, had come into existence; but in the mind of Augustine, not of Pelagius' (p. 345).

[12] Etienne Gilson, *The Christian philosophy of Saint Augustine*, (trans. L.E.M. Lynch) London: Gollancz, 1961, 4: 'the Sceptic or Academician (...) is always in search of truth. He wants to find it; he would like to discover it, but according to his own teaching, this is impossible (...) for him, therefore, happiness is impossible'.

[13] The influence of the Neoplatonists, and particularly Plotinus, upon Augustine and therefore through him on 'Christian philosophy' is an important aspect of this study. Gilson quotes the *City of God* for Augustine's views on 'Neoplatonism': 'These philosophers, then, whom we see deservedly exalted above the rest in fame and glory, have seen that God is not a body, and therefore they have transcended all bodies in search of God, they have seen that whatever is changeable is not the most high God' (*Christian philosophy*, 105). However, as Chadwick points out: 'Augustine also became one of the most penetrating of all critics of this philosophical tradition to which he himself owed so much' (*Augustine*, 3).

[14] Peter Brown, *Religion and society in the age of Saint Augustine*, London: Faber and Faber, 1973, 13.

[15] *Ibid.*, 20.

On the one hand it was a society in which life was tenuous, that faced the possibility of famine every winter if crops should fail; on the other, its very survival had created common bonds: 'By AD 400, the Roman Empire had survived over four hundred such winters. For the Empire had become part of daily life. It was bathed in the elusive glow of shared sentiments, of unquestioned loyalties, of those half-sensed images of security and of the good life that guided the interests of its governing classes'.[16]

It is perhaps what Possidius had in mind when he used the term 'Romania', a new term that had recently come into colloquial use to denote the Roman world, with its characteristic civilisation and way of life as distinct from the barbarian world.[17] Peter Brown expresses it aptly: 'The Spaniards have a word for it, when they describe the bonds of affection in a married couple – 'ilusión', where the elements that made up 'ilusión' changed in the Late Antique period, the Empire itself changed'.[18]

The subterranean changes which were permeating society are perhaps reflected in Augustine's inner development. The curiosity, which gave his intellect its remarkable energy, was also turned upon himself: 'We would not trust a man who had not scrutinized so minutely and with such evident impatience of stereotypes, the strands of his feelings, nor sensed so acutely the gulf between the hidden, unplumbed world within a man, and the opaque, noisy, supremely inquisitive throng of mankind outside it'.[19]

There will be occasions later to look at Augustine's discourse on Psalm XLII in a different context.[20] In it he also reveals that sense of puzzlement with which he looked not only into himself but into others:

> If by 'abyss' we understand a great depth, is man's heart, do you not suppose, 'an abyss'? For what is there more profound than that 'abyss'? Men may speak, may be seen by the operations of their members, may be heard speaking in conversation: but whose thought is penetrated, whose heart seen into? What he is inwardly engaged on, what he is inwardly capable of, what he is inwardly doing or what purposing, what he is inwardly wishing to happen, or not to happen, who shall comprehend?[21]

Some other products of this inner reflection contain the substance of his spirituality. In the *Confessions* he traces the story of his own conversion to the life of

---

[16] *Ibid.*, 16.

[17] Hoare, *Western Fathers*, 232: n.2.

[18] Brown, *Religion and society in the age of Saint Augustine*, 16.

[19] *Ibid.*, 10.

[20] Lat. XLI.

[21] St Augustine, *Discourses on the Psalms*, (see fn.7 above), XLII,12. See also Brown, *Augustine of Hippo*, 172, quotes from *Conf.* IV, 14, 22: 'who can map out the various forces at play in one soul, the different kinds of love (...) Man is a great depth, 0 Lord; you number his hairs, but the hairs of his head are lesser by far to count than his feelings, the movements of his heart'.

faith. In *De Trinitate* he turns into himself to search for the image of God which is the key to the object of faith.

The grafting of Judaeo-Christian tradition with the Hellenic was a major factor in the development of Augustine's spiritual teaching and in his philosophy. The close links between 'philosophy' and 'religion' were characteristic of the Hellenic tradition and facilitated the bridge-building which Augustine achieved. Robert Markus has well described the characteristic:

> Even on the level at which philosophy was pursued by creative thinkers like Plotinus, the goals of philosophy were akin to those of religion. Men looked to philosophy for an explanatory scheme of the world, of man and of God. And in catering for this longing, philosophy came increasingly to mean the quest of God. Its activity might culminate in a union or a vision which we might be tempted to call 'mystical'. Moreover, in the Greco-Roman world philosophy was often seen as a way of life (…) The philosophic life in general was held to imply a break with accepted norms of conduct; asceticism, self-denial and renunciation of worldliness went with it. The image of the philosopher is one of the ideal types venerated in Antiquity and provided Christianity with a type for the saint. Conversion to philosophy was perhaps the nearest the ancient world came to approaching the idea of conversion to Christianity.[22]

Justin tells us his conversion to Christianity was a conversion to philosophy.[23] Christians were aware that their religion offered a synthesis of what were generally two separate things in the ancient world. Augustine thought that Christianity alone had brought a resolution of the ancient tensions between cult and philosophy.[24] Pagan philosophy had often been very cool towards popular religion: 'For the educated pagan the popular cults were often no more than a clumsy means of embodying the truths of philosophy on a level accessible to the common run of men'.[25]

Religious traditions could be read as allegories of the hidden truth uncovered by the learned. Augustine's fusion of revelation and philosophy in fact turned this notion on its head. For him philosophy became the handmaid of Christian religious tradition.

How did Augustine achieve this fusion? For an answer to this question we may first turn to his 'conversion', for it was in those months between his experience 'in the garden' and 'the vision of Ostia' that he realised, in both senses of the word, his Christian vocation.

---

[22] Robert Markus, *Christianity in the Roman world*, London: Thames & Hudson, 1974, 39.

[23] *Ibid.*, 40. Justin Martyr (c. AD 100 – c. AD 165).

[24] St Augustine, *De vera religione*, V, 8 in: *Augustine: Earlier writings* (ed. J.H.S. Burleigh), Philadelphia: Library of Christian Classics, 1953, 230.

[25] Markus, *Christianity in the Roman world*, 40.

Augustine's 'Conversion'

Augustine's conversion began with a prolonged preparatory induction in which he was attracted to the idea of 'philosophy' as the pursuit of 'wisdom' and, retrospectively, saw the providential hand of God.[26] There seem to have been two equally important components in his Christian conversion. The first was that he had been directly spoken to by God, called by Him. This happened in the Milan garden setting, after much heart searching and indecision, when the call was mediated by a child's voice.[27] The second was an appropriation of the call as an 'ascent to God' and as a surpassingly beautiful and enlightening experience. This realisation was cemented in his mind by the recollection of the 'vision of Ostia'.[28]

Serge Lancel in his biography of Augustine has treated the process of conversion as two phases, 'intellectual' and 'moral'.[29] Intellectual conversion is concerned with the process by which he became convinced that the Christian Church embodied the ultimate 'Truth'. Moral conversion was the process by which Augustine decided to become a Christian and change his lifestyle dramatically. Both phases are processes even if marked by particular events.

Lancel's characterisation of two processes, 'intellectual' preceding 'moral' conversion, is in a different sequence from the events which Augustine described in the *Confessions*. There the 'garden' experience marked the 'moral' turning, the active phase. The 'Ostia' experience vitalised the 'intellectual' turning, the contemplative phase, by enabling Augustine to understand his 'Christianisation', as a personal appropriation, in 'Neoplatonic' terms.

He understood his 'Ostia' experience as a turning inwards and a journey of ascent much in the manner of Plotinus who had also experienced moments of surpassing enlightenment. Augustine uses similar images to those used by Plotinus in the *Enneads*. Such moments revitalise the efforts to enjoy the ultimate beatitude and fire the 'anagogic imagination'.

However, Augustine also emphasises that all his own efforts, whether 'intellectual' or 'moral', are dependent on the mercy of God in the revelation of His Son and in the redemption which Christ's crucifixion secured. His experience of his own powerlessness to effect his own conversion initiated his exploration of Christian teaching. His act of faith in receiving Baptism was a new beginning. It was a merciful God alone who had descended to pull him out of the mire of doubt and indecision and enabled him to advance.

---

[26] St Augustine, *Confessions*, III, 4, 7.
[27] *Ibid.*, VIII, 8,19.
[28] *Ibid.*, IX,10,23-24.
[29] Serge Lancel (*St Augustine*, London: SCM Press, 2002), discusses Augustine's conversion in chapters X and XI as 'Intellectual' and 'Of the Will' respectively.

The Christian faith provided the power for his conversion while his under-standing of Neoplatonic method, which he discovered in his Milanese circle of acquaintanceships, provided the framework within which he could understand his faith.[30] Augustine discovered the Christian God in the cultural milieu in which his pre-Christian career had developed. He never forgot the Christian influences who had mediated his discovery; the role of his mother, Monica,[31] in his conversion, or the other direct influences, Ambrose,[32] Simplicianus,[33] Pon-ticianus and the story of St Anthony of Egypt[34] and that of Victorinus[35] and, perhaps above all, St Paul.[36] In retrospect he realised how dependent he had been on the experience of the Church. The realisation inspired his subsequent career as priest and bishop.

Augustine's experience of conversion coloured the spirituality of his faith and put a personal stamp upon it that coloured the spirituality of the mediaeval Church. It is this personal stamp that is recognised when we speak of 'Augus-tinianism' to which we will now turn.

The Characteristics of Augustine's 'Christian Philosophy'

Augustine's 'Christian philosophy', as Gilson has aptly called it in his great work[37], is not a system, that is a collection of truths ready-made and linked together in an order in which they may be understood and remembered. His writings provide a method; an order to follow in a long series of efforts which each individual must make to understand their destiny and how to reach it. This is why his 'philosophy' is so closely linked to his spirituality. The pursuit of 'sapi-entia' is the ascent to God. In his writings: 'Not a single idea is defined with thor-ough metaphysical strictness, not a single technical term keeps the same mean-ing from the beginning to end. There are conjectures and adumbrations everywhere, attempts made again and again and soon abandoned only to appear once more just when we felt they had been forgotten'.[38]

If, however, his approach is treated as a method, everything takes on a differ-ent appearance; the gaps become so many fields left open to the free play of inner

---

[30] *Ibid.*, 82-84.
[31] St Augustine, *Confessions*, IX, 8-13, 17-36.
[32] *Ibid.*, VI, 3, 3.
[33] *Ibid.*, VIII, 1, 1.
[34] *Ibid.*, VIII, 6, 13.
[35] *Ibid.*, VIII, 2, 3-5, and 9.
[36] *Ibid.*, VII, 21, 27.
[37] Gilson, *Christian philosophy*. The following discussion of Augustine's philosphy is based on this brilliant analysis.
[38] *Ibid.*, 245.

development, and it is recognised that it is for the individual to fill the gaps. This attitude agrees with the fundamental conditions Augustine set for all philosophical teaching and enquiry: 'For, he has shown that nothing passes from one mind into another. No one ever learns anything. Each man sees the truth common to all only to the extent that it becomes the truth of his own mind'.[39]

His writings, not only in their internal logical development but in their totality, reflect challenges being faced and tackled by the application of a characteristic method; a method which always takes the reader back to the fundamental premises about human destiny as reflected in the Christian revelation. The range of problems Augustine faced test and prove his method and give his works the range and depth of a great 'Summa' but without the logical interconnections.

The challenges Augustine faced were not only external but also internal or personal. His philosophical method reflects the profound impact which his own experience had upon him. His philosophy has been aptly called 'a metaphysics of inner experience'.[40] 'He is a man yearning to be self-sufficient'[41] but unable to do without God. Gilson suggests that this is the key to his doctrine; and that the obscure forces which give rise to the struggle 'are to be found in every human heart' and reveal 'the pride and misery of everyone of us'.[42] This is the source not only of Augustine's extraordinary individuality but also his 'universality': 'We have here a philosophical vision combined with a religious experience and the two cannot be separated without falsifying arbitrarily the testimony of Augustine himself'.[43]

Augustine not only provided a way of understanding religious experience but also the notion that the most sublime religious experience, that of 'the vision of God', was the goal most to be desired in this life.

The themes which colour Augustine's spirituality tend to be those which characterise his philosophy. Gilson has analysed the characteristics of 'Augustinianism' in philosophy.[44] It is proposed to review these briefly and then relate them to Augustine's spiritual teaching from those sources where perhaps the most complete picture can be obtained; from the *Confessions, De Trinitate,* and the

---

[39] *Ibid.*

[40] *Ibid.,* 240. Quoted from W. Windelband, *Geschichte der Philosophie*, Tübingen 1910, 230ff.

[41] *Ibid.*

[42] *Ibid.*

[43] *Ibid.,* 233.

[44] *Ibid.,* 227-246. See also 364: fn. 49. 'There was a psychological evolution in St Augustine; there were many variations in detail and a great number of these we have pointed out, but we have never discovered the slightest philosophical change in any of his essential theses. St Augustine fixed his main ideas from the time of his conversion – even, we believe, regarding grace – and he always drew on the capital he had acquired. It goes without saying that a study of the changes in Augustine, wherever they occurred, has its importance, but its point of view is different from, and complementary to ours'.

Discourses on the Psalms. They also reflect the range of his religious moods – the introverted, the speculative and the mystical/lyrical.[45]

Turning first to the characteristics which Gilson suggests reflect 'Augustinianism' in philosophy; there are six of these.

The first and fundamental idea is that there can be no true philosophy without an act of adherence to the supernatural order which frees the will from the flesh through grace and the mind from scepticism through revelation. In other words, an act of faith is required; *'credo ut intellegam'*: 'Augustine's doctrine proclaims the insufficiency of philosophy on every page'.[46] The origins of this notion lie in Augustine's two basic psychological insights; that humans need to obtain absolute certitude, and so must look to finding the 'unchangeable' if they are to attain peace and happiness. The corollary is that it is not sufficient to establish only the ideological framework for faith, but that humans must also find a rule of life so that the mind can secure control over the senses. In Gilson's words: 'Without Christ the mediator who became flesh to liberate us from the flesh, without the revelation of scripture which determines with transcendent authority the body of salutary truths, man can only wander aimlessly at the whim of concupiscence and vacillate between antagonistic systems'.[47]

The second postulate is that the energising force around which all doctrine is constructed is the love of God – the concept of charity. The motivation for action should be the love of God because creation was an act of love. Gilson suggests that this notion accounts for much of the discursive element in Augustine's writings: 'If we are dealing not so much with knowledge but with love then the philosopher's task is not so much to cause knowledge as to cause love. Now in order to arouse love we do not prove we show'.[48]

Or as Pascal puts it, 'Jesus Christ and St Paul follow the order of charity, not that of intellect, because they wanted to warm rather than instruct. It is the same with St Augustine'.[49] In Gilson's view the more a doctrine is centred on 'charity' the more 'Augustinian' it is.[50]

A third idea is that the 'natural' human being is the 'fallen' being. Augustine is aware of human limitations: 'An Augustinian doctrine will incline spontaneously towards that which concedes less to nature and more to God'.[51] Augustine reconciles, though this is not his explicit purpose, the Platonic cosmology

---

[45] *Ibid.*, 236, fn.50. P. Monceaux, *Histoire de la litterature latine chrétienne*, Paris: Payot, 1924, 137.
[46] *Ibid.*, 235.
[47] *Ibid.*
[48] *Ibid.*, 236.
[49] *Ibid.*, fn.50. Quoted from B. Pascal, *Pensées* (ed. L. Brunschvicg).
[50] *Ibid.*, 240.
[51] *Ibid.*

with its motionless world of essences and the Judaeo-Christian cosmology with its history of the world and humanity. He develops a historical cosmology whose perspectives always lead him to describe how God communicated himself to nature and humanity through creation: How after the order established by that communication was destroyed by sin, a second nature replaced the first; how finally the original order could be restored. Thus the nature Augustine is examining is the historical remains of a divine order corrupted by sin. By contrast St Thomas Aquinas regards nature as a 'metaphysically indestructible essence, whose intrinsic necessity resists even the corruption of original sin and surrenders to it only the graces removed by it and the powers weakened or vitiated by it'. The two views are not irreconcilable in Gilson's view and the 'likeness' which Augustine seeks to restore in *De Trinitate* by destroying the 'image of sin' seems to reconcile the two views.[52] However, Augustine 'reduces the world's history to the history of sin and grace' because he thinks of the cosmic drama in terms of that enacted within his own soul. In his description of nature and man he is always guided by the powerful experience of his own conversion.[53]

In view of the recurring debate about the roles of faith and reason throughout the Middle Ages, the fourth characteristic is of particular importance; the idea that revelation is a 'source of light' for the reason. Despite the theocentric orientation of the other postulates, Augustine does not disparage the function or power of reason. On the contrary, reason is the means by which revelation can be understood. As Gilson aptly put it:

> In a genuinely Augustinian doctrine faith points out, it does not prove. It is one thing to begin with something revealed as the theologian does, so as to define it or rationally deduce its content, and it is quite another to begin with something revealed, as the Augustinian does when he philosophises, to see whether and to what extent its content coincides with the content of reason.[54]

The fifth mark of 'Augustinianism' is its refusal to count as 'true philosophy' any doctrine which shows what must be done but fails to provide the power to do it, *beati ergo qui factis et moribus cantant canticum graduum*[55] ('happy are they who rise to him in word and thought, but blessed are they whose very life and actions sing the canticle of the steps'.). 'Augustinianism' is an ascent to God. However, Augustine refuses to separate speculation and action in the pursuit of beatitude.[56] This point illustrates the gulf which exists between Augustine and the Greek philosophers from whom he drew inspiration: 'Plotinus sees the truth

---

[52] *Ibid.*
[53] *Ibid.*
[54] *Ibid.*, 242.
[55] *Ibid.* Quoted from *De Trinitate*, XI.6.
[56] *Ibid.*, that is to translate the vision of contemplation into action.

and longs for it; Porphyry knows that philosophy's task is the liberation of the soul and he bends to it with a will; but neither knows the only way which leads to the goal, namely Jesus Christ, the model and well-spring of humanity'.[57]

The final idea is basic to the concept of spirituality. It arises from Augustine's concern to ensure that people are aware of the limits of their own powers so that it will be easier for them to effect their own conversion; to turn back towards God. His objective, derived from his Platonic inheritance, is to establish the primacy of spirit over matter – the soul's basic transcendence over the body. It is vital for people to know that the greatest goods belong to the order of the spirit. A series of closely linked propositions follow from Augustine's views on sensible things, which Gilson suggests were rarely to be separated during the course of history.[58]

It is the Platonic inspiration in Augustine's thought which gives it the ambiance of philosophic mysticism. Nevertheless, the biblical influence directs its application and direction:

> To Plotinus he is indebted for almost all the matter and for the whole technique of his philosophy. He is indebted to the Bible for the basic Christian notions which compelled him to make the inner transformations he performed on the Plotinian thesis he borrowed and to construct in this way a new doctrine which represents one of the first, and one of the most original, contributions Christianity has made to enrich the history of philosophy.[59]

From this synthesis emerge the principal themes which determine the development and style of both his own spirituality and that of others.

The themes, as they have emerged from the discussion of the key characteristics of his philosophical approach, may be broadly classified as those relating to the nature of human beings on the one hand, and their relationship with God on the other. Human nature is spiritual. Created in God's image, the likeness has been obscured by 'the fall' from grace. The natural human is now fallen being dependent on God, through Christ as mediator, for the restoration of the original likeness which constitutes the only true goal of human life. Life must be directed towards this end and the eventual reunion with God. Augustine's

---

[57] *Ibid.*

[58] *Ibid.*, 243-245. These important propositions may be summarised as follows: 'Since the Soul radically transcends the body it must be impervious to the body'. This is what Gilson calls 'the principle of the innerness of mind' because a whole series of consequences follow from the view that nothing enters the Augustinian soul from without; it receives nothing which is prior to itself and so the 'soul itself is the soul's first object'. Since nothing separates the thinking subject from the object of thought, the Augustinian soul discovers invincible certitude and a guarantee of the possibility of certitude in general 'in the very act whereby it apprehends itself'. See also Frederick Coppleston, *A history of philosophy;* vol.2, part 1, New York: Image Books, 1962, 66-82.

[59] *Ibid.*, 234.

spiritual teaching is directed to this end; it is a formula for living predicated on these ideological premises. However, the tensions which arise from this analysis create the themes which dominate the debate about the nature of the spiritual life; the tensions between the contemplative and active lives, between love and knowledge of God, between humans as the image of sin and their potentiality to be like God, between grace and freedom and between faith and reason, – the respective roles of God and the human being in the quest for God. These antitheses form the agenda for continuing debate.

Before turning to the particular works to be discussed, Augustine's views on the issue of the contemplative and active lives, which is a recurring theme in the future, creates the scenario within which thought about the spiritual life develops. The issue is never far from the surface in the *De Civitate Dei* in the form of the claims of the *vita otiosa* (contemplative life) and *vita negotiosa*[60] (active life):

> So whereas the study of wisdom is either concerning action or contemplation and thence assumes two several names, active and contemplative, the active consisting in the practice of morality in one's life, and the contemplative in penetrating into the abstruse causes of nature and the nature of divinity.[61]

His interpretation of the allegories of the wives of Jacob, Lea and Rachel[62] and of Martha and Mary,[63] lead him to the conclusion that the contemplative life has primacy. He refers to it in unequivocal terms:

> The going to God, that is the very contemplation of Truth (…) the striving to grasp intellectually those things which truly and supremely are, is the highest act of seeing (aspectus) of the soul, than which it has none more perfect or better.[64]

How does Augustine reconcile the nature of such spiritual pursuits with the realities of corporeal existence? He says of the carrying on of human affairs:

> Wherefore the love of truth requires a holy retiredness; and the necessity of charity a just employment, which if it be not imposed upon us, we ought not to seek,

---

[60] St Augustine, *De civitate Dei*, (trans. John Healy) London: Dent, 1950, vol.II, bk. xix, chap. xix, 256, 257. 'But as concerning the three kinds of life, active, contemplative, and the mean between both, although one may keep the faith in any of those courses, yet there is a difference between the love of the truth and the duties of charity. One may not be so given to contemplation that he neglect the good of his neighbour, nor so far in love with action that he forgot divine speculation'.

[61] St Augustine, *De civitate Dei*, vol.I, bk. viii, chap. iv, 228.

[62] C. Butler, *Western mysticism*, London: Constable, 1967, 52-58, quotes Augustine, *C. Faust.*, xxii.

[63] *Ibid.*, quotes Augustine *Sermons*, ciii, civ, clxix, cciv.

[64] *Ibid.*, 74,75, quotes Augustine *De quant. anima*.

but betake ourselves wholly to the holy search after truth; but if we be called forth unto a position, the law and need of charity binds us to undertake it. Yet we may not for all this give over our first resolve of contemplation, lest we lose its sweetness, and be surcharged with the weight of the other.[65]

His attitude to contemplation in his own life reveals that ambiance of philosophic mysticism, already referred to. Speaking of contemplation:

> This I often do, this delights me, and as far as I may be freed from necessary duties, unto this pleasure have I recourse (…) And sometimes thou admittest me to an affection, very unusual, in my inmost soul; rising to a strange sweetness, which if it were perfected in me, I know not what in it would not belong to the life to come.[66]

Augustine's idea of 'contemplation', as an 'ascent to God', is well illustrated by his treatment in the *Confessions* and *De Trinitate*. In the *Confessions*, the act of contemplation is seen as the goal, the end of a search; in *De Trinitate*, it is seen as the beginning of the search. Between them these two approaches also reveal the twin thrusts of Augustine's search for God, through love and knowledge. The *Confessions* is highly affective in mood, while De *Trinitate* is characteristically speculative.

The *Confessions*

In the *Confessions* Augustine's starting point is the phenomenon of human restlessness which he illustrates from his own experience of the path to faith and conversion: 'In his hands [Augustine's] this longing for God is transformed from a human restlessness to our response to the incredible love and condescension of God, indeed is the movement of the Holy Spirit Himself in our hearts'.[67]

Right at the beginning of the *Confessions* the leitmotiv, which gives the work its theme and its great beauty emerges:

> Thou hast made us for Thyself and our hearts are restless till they rest in thee.[68]

This is the guiding principle of Augustine's mystical theology. The vision of Ostia left a deep impression on Augustine. It was experienced quite early in the post-conversion period and provided him with a foretaste of what 'resting in

---

[65] St Augustine, *De civitate Dei*, vol. II, bk.xix, chap.xix, 257.

[66] St Augustine, *Confessions*, X, 40, 65.

[67] Andrew Louth, *The origins of the Christian mystical tradition from Plato to Dionysus*, Oxford: Oxford University Press, 1985, 134.

[68] St Augustine, *Confessions*, I,1,1.

Thee' could mean. The Plotinian influence is clearly evident in the way he describes what he experienced:

> Rising as our love flamed upward towards that self- same, we passed in review the various levels of bodily things, up to the heavens themselves, where sun and moon and stars shine upon this earth. And higher still we soared, thinking in our minds and speaking and marvelling at your works: and so we came to our own souls, and went beyond them to come at last to that region of richness unending (...)[69]

It is essentially a fleeting experience, a foretaste of the joys of heaven. It is not a full revelation of God either; yet he does not rule out the possibility entirely. As Ladner points out, 'Without limiting the essential vision of God on earth in principle Augustine never names anyone except Moses and St Paul as having possessed it'.[70]

In this regard he parts company with the Greeks.

> For the Greeks it was the great goal of all mystical experience, though according to them, it could be had, even in heaven, not in final attainment, but only in never-ending pursuit... The Greeks could not imagine any vision of God as 'satisfactory' because the essential vision to them meant comprehensive union, whereas in the Western tradition there can be a true, though not a full vision of God in this life, with fulfilment in the beatific vision in heaven.[71]

The tension between the ideas of 'grace' and 'human volition' is revealed in the way in which the goal of human life is viewed. On the one hand it can be viewed as the natural culmination of a human longing for God or on the other as something that God gives; 'The former is the line taken by Platonism and it is reinforced by the Platonic idea that the soul is returning to the divine realm in its ascent, that it is going back home. The latter is characteristically Christian and is something that Augustine progressively makes his own in his understanding of the soul's way to God'.[72]

---

[69] *Ibid.*, IX, 10, 24. Louth (*Origins*, 139) compares Augustine's description with Plotinus' *Ennead* V,14: 'Admiring the world of sense as we look upon its vastness and beauty and the order of its eternal march, thinking of the gods within it, seen and hidden, and the celestial spirits and all the life of animal and plant, let us mount to its archetype, to the yet more authentic sphere'. The standard edition of Plotinus used by Louth is P. Henry and H.R. Schwyzer, *Plotini Opera*, 3 vols (Paris-Brussels, 1951-73). The translation used is Plotinus: *The Enneads*, by Stephen MacKenna, rev. by B.S. Page (London, 1969).

[70] G.B. Ladner, *The idea of reform: Its impact on Christian thought and action in the age of the Fathers*, Cambridge, Mass.: Harvard University Press, 1959, 191: fn.18, quoted by Louth *Origins*, 138.

[71] Louth, *Origins*, 138.

[72] *Ibid.*, 141.

The Platonic idea has the element of predestination about it; the Christian idea which is Augustine's is that God reveals Himself, in however limited a way, but has to be also invited to do so.[73] It is in the conjunction on the one hand of desire, or love, of humans for God and on the other God's gift of Himself, that the element of tension arises in the Christian idea as interpreted by Augustine. As was noticed in discussing the characteristics of Augustine's philosophy, he tends to attribute more to God and less to humans.

The Platonic notion of the soul's return to God, as if impelled by some homing instinct in its nature, nevertheless had considerable influence upon Augustine. As Paul Henry put it, '...it was the 'desire for God' in the philosophy of Plotinus, the echo in the Enneads of 'fecisti nos ad te' – 'thou hast made us for Thyself' – which caught the heart of the son of Monica; it was the conformity of the Platonist doctrine of the Logos with the teaching of the Church on the Word, preached by Ambrose.[74]

When Augustine begins his search for God in the tenth book of the *Confessions,* he goes to the memory. *Memoria* for Augustine is the whole mind, both conscious and unconscious, not just the faculty of recollection. There he will investigate Plotinus' mysterious homing signal which has close affinities with the biblical notion of the image of God in humanity and also the recollection of the 'unending richness' which he experienced in the vision of Ostia. The former he will return to in *De Trinitate* the latter he pursues in the *Confessions.* He begins with a question of himself, the technique of introspection which becomes so familiar in Augustine's work:

> What is it that I love when I love You? Not the beauty of any bodily thing, not the order of the seasons, not the brightness of the light that rejoices the eye, nor the sweet melodies of all songs, nor the sweet fragrance of flowers and ointments and spices; not manna or honey, not the limbs that carnal love embraces. None of these things do I love in loving my God. Yet in a sense I do love light and melody and fragrance and food and embrace when I love my God – the light and the voice and the fragrance and the food and embrace in the soul, when that light shines upon my soul which no place can contain, that voice sounds which no time can take from me, I breathe that fragrance which no wind scatters, I eat the food which is not lessened by eating, and I lie in the embrace which satiety never comes to sunder. This it is that I love, when I love my God.[75]

---

[73] Brown, *Augustine of Hippo*, 176, interprets Augustine's view from *de lib.arbr.* as follows: 'Man's first awareness, therefore, must be of a need to be healed; but this meant both accepting responsibility for what one is, and at one and the same time, welcoming dependence on a therapy beyond one's control'.

[74] Louth, *Origins*, 149, quotes P. Henry, *La vision d'Ostie*, Paris 1938, 77.

[75] St Augustine, *Confessions*, X, 6, 8.

It is the experience of the enjoyment of God which encompasses the whole range of enjoyments which corporeal existence provides. But more than this; it is 'unending' enjoyment which cannot be dulled by satiation. The experience of God is felt inwardly, but it still does not answer the question, 'what is this God?' There follows the famous passage in which Augustine examines creation which points beyond itself, saying it is not God. So he rises above the material creation by entering into himself, into his soul which gives life and sense to his body and has made possible the very seeing and examining that he is engaged in:

> I ask again what it is that I love when I love my God? Who is He that is above the topmost point of my soul? By that same soul I shall ascend to Him.[76]

And,

> I shall mount beyond this power of my nature still rising by degrees towards Him who made me. And so I come to the fields and vast palaces of memory...[77]

The first step to God is discovery of self, discovery of self as a spiritual being that contains and transcends the material order:

> You are not the mind itself, because you are the Lord God of the mind, and all those things suffer change, but You remain unchangeable over all; and yet You deign to dwell in my memory ever since the time I first learned of You.[78]

The realisation of God's condescension in deigning to dwell in the memory[79] produces one of the great lyrical passages in the *Confessions*:

> Late have I loved Thee, O Beauty, so ancient and so new; late have I loved Thee! For behold Thou wert within me and I was not with Thee. I was kept from Thee by those things, yet had they not been in Thee, they would not have been at all. Thou didst call and cry to me and break open my deafness: And Thou didst send forth thy beams and shine upon me and chase away my blindness: Thou didst breathe fragrance upon me and I drew in my breath and now I do pant for Thee: I tasted Thee, and now hunger and thirst for Thee: Thou didst touch me, and I have burned for Thy peace.[80]

---

[76] *Ibid.*, X, 7, 11.

[77] *Ibid.*, X, 8, 12.

[78] *Ibid.*, X, 25, 36.

[79] The significance of the memory for Augustine is well brought out by Brown in discussing Augustine's conversion, *Augustine of Hippo*, 174: 'when Augustine struggles with himself in the garden, what is at stake is no generalised "force of evil", no extraneous "matter" that had "splashed mud" on the pure metal of the soul; it is a tension in the very memory itself, a battle with the precise quality of past experiences: "Habit was only too strong for me when it asked: Do you think you can do without these things?"' (*Conf.* VIII,11,26.)

[80] St Augustine, *Confessions*, X,27,38.

God is recognised not as one who can be found but as one who discloses Himself in the soul, like a beam of light – that soul which depends on Him for its very existence. The disclosure is received as grace:

> All my hope is naught save in Thy great mercy, grant what Thou commandest, and command what Thou wilt.[81]

The emphasis on grace and on God's active intervention takes Augustine beyond Plotinus' conception of the 'One' as disinterested and impersonal. Augustine's God is intensely personal:

> Thou dost command continence (…) For by continence we are all collected and bound up into unity within ourself, whereas we had been scattered abroad in multiplicity. Too little does any man love Thee, who loves some other thing together with Thee, loving it not on account of Thee. 0 Thou Love, who art ever burning and never extinguished! 0 charity, my God, enkindle me! Thou dost command continence: grant what Thou dost command and command what Thou wilt.[82]

By 'continence' Augustine means single-minded devotion to God. For the remainder of Book X he examines himself to see how far he measures up to that command. This quest leads him to the doctrine of the Mediator. Without God's condescension to us in the Incarnation to respond to, in Augustine's view, humans will either despair because of the consciousness of unworthiness or seek God under the inspiration of pride. Humans can only achieve purity of heart, the elimination of all loves but love of God, through humility. This can only be awakened in their hearts by the love of God in the Incarnation:

> But the true Mediator, whom in the secret of Your mercy You have shown to man and sent to men, that by this example they might learn humility – the Mediator between God and man, the man Christ Jesus, appeared between sinful mortals and the immortal Just One (…) Rightly is my hope strong in Him, who sits at Thy right hand and intercedes for us; otherwise I should despair for many and great are my infirmities, many and great; but Thy medicine is of more power. We might well have thought Thy Word remote from union with man and so despaired of ourselves, if He had not been made flesh and dwelt among us.[83]

So Augustine proclaims the insufficiency of philosophy to satisfy the longing in his own heart for 'Truth' and 'Wisdom'. The 'Truth' can only be sought in the Word made flesh and found through God's grace as he discloses Himself in the individual Soul.

---

[81]   *Ibid.*, X, 29, 40.
[82]   *Ibid.*
[83]   *Ibid.*, X, 43, 68.

De Trinitate

In the *Confessions* Augustine has explored his own experience of the search for 'Truth'.[84] If he proclaims the insufficiency of philosophic reasoning, he by no means rejects it. In *De Trinitate* he illustrates the manner in which reason can be used to understand the truths of revelation and explore what God has revealed of Himself. In the *Confessions* Augustine shows himself in the role of apologist;[85] in *De Trinitate* it is the speculative Augustine that appears.

The experience of Ostia has caused Augustine to put behind him the question of the nature of God as an intellectual puzzle. His quest in *De Trinitate* is to understand that experience so that he may extend it. The fleeting glimpse of 'unending richness' has not so much brought him peace as quickened his desire to enjoy it more fully. It is a desire that he pursues, however, with the confidence that it will be fulfilled. The question he raises in *De Trinitate* is how it will be fulfilled.

In the first seven books of *De Trinitate* he attempts to establish from Scripture what God has revealed of Himself. And God has revealed himself as Trinity. In the latter half of *De Trinitate* he moves on from what he believes – understands in that sense – to how the soul can come to contemplate the God in whom it believes.[86] The latter half of *De Trinitate* is therefore concerned with the soul's ascent to God – the very essence of his spirituality. The key point in his understanding of the soul's ascent to God is his doctrine that the soul is created in the image and likeness of God. Augustine's insight is to reject as 'subordinationist' the received doctrine. The Son, the Word of God, is not the image of God; He is God.[87] Therefore, the human cannot be the image of the Image of God. For Augustine the image of God is the human, or to be more precise, the human's rational soul. Since God is Trinity, the image of God in the human

---

[84] 'For behold, You have taken delight in truth; and he that does truth comes to the light. I desire to do truth in my heart, before Thee, by confession: with my pen, before many witnesses'. (*Conf.*, X,1,1).

[85] Chadwick, *Augustine*, 68: 'In so far as the work had a polemical target, it was directed against the Manichees'.

[86] *Ibid.*, 91. 'The two halves corresponded to his antithesis between faith and understanding'.

[87] *Ibid.* 'Arius had precipitated a major controversy by his thesis that the doctrine of the divine Triad could be reconciled with monotheism by conceding, or indeed insisting on, the metaphysical and moral subordination of the Son to the Father. Augustine felt, with some reason, that the anti-Arian arguments of orthodox writers, including even the best Greek theologians of the fourth century, had been less effective and forceful than they should have been (...) The orthodox tradition rejected not only Arius, but also the rival notion, associated with an obscure third century heretic named Sabellius, that Father, Son and Spirit are adjectival terms expressing attributes of the One God. In short, it [the orthodox tradition] rejected the idea that Father, Son and Spirit are merely adjectives or full substantives'.

soul must be Trinitarian: He makes the point in commenting on the text from Genesis; 'Let us make man after our image, in our likeness':

> For why the 'our' if the Son is the image of the Father alone? But it is on account of the imperfect likeness, as we have said, that man is spoken of as 'after the image', and so 'our', that man might be an image of the Trinity; not equal to the Trinity, as the Son to the Father, but approaching it, as is said, by a certain likeness; as in things distinct there can be closeness, not however in this case spatially, but by imitation.[88]

The search for the soul's return to God is in two parts. Books VIII-X of *De Trinitate* are about the true nature of humankind – their Trinitarian nature; the later books establish how the image of God in the human can be turned to Him so that it can truly reflect Him and know Him most deeply. Augustine is less concerned in Books VIII-X to illustrate the doctrine of Trinity from his understanding of humanity than to discover the true nature of the human from what he knows of the doctrine of the Trinity which he believes by faith: He finds the Trinitarian image of God in the spiritual properties of the mind; memory, understanding and will:

> Now this triad of memory, understanding and will are not three lives, but one; nor three minds but one (…) And these three constitute one thing, one life, one mind, one essence.[89]

There is a completely co-equal trinity in the mind, each member of the trinity entirely co-penetrates the others, there is complete co-inherence. So a true image of God in the mind has been identified.

The next stage is the return of this image to its archetype, God. This is a process, not simply an act: The soul must learn what it means to be the image of God in its memory, understanding and will, and then learn how to pass beyond the image to God Himself in contemplation of Him. The problem is how the soul can free itself from being tied to the external world and the change and corruption associated with it. The distinction is made between *scientia*, knowledge concerned with action in the world, and *sapientia*, that concerned with eternal reality and contemplation of it. The problem is transposed to understanding how the soul may move from *scientia* to *sapientia*.[90] Before the 'Fall' the soul knew *sapientia*, but as a consequence of it, it now only knows *scientia* – 'the soul loving its own power' – has slipped from what is universal and common to what is private and partial. Book XIII describes how the soul can free itself from the effects of the 'Fall'. That is only possible as a result of faith in the

---

[88] St Augustine, *De Trinitate*, VII, 6,12.
[89] *Ibid.*, X,18,11.
[90] Louth, *Origins*, 153.

Incarnation. As St Paul says, 'all the treasures of wisdom and knowledge' are hidden in the Incarnate Lord – both 'scientia' which humans can reach, and 'sapientia' which they want to reach:

> Our 'Scientia' is Christ, our 'Sapientia' is the same Christ. He introduces among us faith concerning things, He shows truth concerning eternal things. Through Him we rise to Him, we pass through scientia to sapientia: we do not, however, move away from the one and the same Christ 'in which are hid all the treasures of wisdom and knowledge'.[91]

Humans must submit to being purified through temporal things; only the humble mind can submit to the Incarnate One, who Himself teaches the way of humility:

> Because it is pride that is the cause of all our sickness which the Son of God came to heal, He descended and was made humble. How can man continue in his pride? God has been made humble for him. It shames you perhaps to imitate a humble man: imitate then the humble God.[92]

In Book XIV Augustine turns to the question of how the image of God is perfected in humans when they contemplate God. The image of the Trinity in the soul is not there because the soul remembers, and knows and loves itself, but because in this it shows its capacity to remember, know and love Him by whom it has been made:

> The mind will be raised to the participation of his being, truth and bliss, though nothing will thereby be added to the being, truth and bliss which is its own in that being, joined to it in perfect happiness, it will have a changeless life and enjoy a changeless vision of all that it will behold.[93]

It is in this cleaving to God through its memory, understanding and will that the soul attains wisdom and thus:

> Wisdom will be the mind's not by its own illumination, but by partaking in that Supreme Light, and only when it enters eternity will it reign in bliss.[94]

Augustine is insistent that it is only by God that the soul can be transformed into God's image:

> The beginning of the image's reforming must come from Him who first formed it. The self which it was able to deform, it cannot itself reform.[95]

---

[91] St Augustine, *De Trinitate* XIII, 24,19.
[92] *Ibid., Tractatus in Joannem,* XXV,16.
[93] *Ibid., De Trinitate,* XIX, 20,14.
[94] *Ibid.,* XIV, 15,12.
[95] *Ibid.,* XIV, 22,16.

It is not only reformation by God, but reformation according to God; reformation into the image of God. This renewal begins in a single moment, the moment of Baptism, but the perfection of the image in the human is the result of a long process:

> The cure's beginning is to remove the cause of sickness: and that is done through the forgiveness of sins. Its furtherance is the healing of the sickness itself, which takes effect by gradual progress in the renewal of the image.[96]

> The image that is being renewed in the spirit of the mind, in the knowledge of God, not outwardly but inwardly from day to day, will be made perfect by that vision, face to face, that shall be after the judgement – the vision which is now but-a-growing, through a glass darkly.[97]

And so the soul returns to God – not in a moment of ecstasy, but in a long process of renewal which will never end in this life, following a way that has been disclosed by the light of the doctrine of the Trinity and in which the Trinity is gradually disclosed in the heart of the Christian. *De Trinitate* provides a fine example of Augustine's philosophic methodology harnessed in the exposition of revealed truth to solve the puzzles of humanity's spiritual destiny. The search for the image of God in the soul and its identification in the spiritual properties of memory, understanding and will as a true representation of the Trinitarian image, lead on to the solution of the problem of restoring the image as the prerequisite for the enjoying the supreme Good, the vision of God. The 'image and likeness' themes are closely linked to those of 'faith' and 'knowledge' and 'grace'. The three latter themes are linked in the idea, 'our Scientia is Christ, our Sapientia is the same Christ'.[98] He is the means by which humanity acquires knowledge of God and the means by which, through faith in Him and the grace of His unseen presence, rises above the pull of the world and adheres to the triune God as He discloses Himself and effects the final purification of the soul which is the concomitant of that vision.

---

[96] *Ibid.*, XIV, 23,17.

[97] *Ibid.*, XIV, 25,19.

[98] The idea is expanded by Chadwick, *Augustine*, 95: 'History he regarded as the object of his worldly knowledge (scientia) quite distinct from higher wisdom (sapientia). But the platonic disjunction of the two worlds of sense and mind could be overcome by applying the Christian concept of history as being like a sacramental ladder which God can use, elevating the soul from the active life to the contemplative, from the temporal to eternal, through the Jesus of history who becomes the Christ of Faith (F.12.26 T.13.24). We are to pass by him on the path to the vision of unchanging eternity (S.88)'. [Chadwick's abbreviations, vi.]

Discourses on the Psalms

In both the *Confessions* and *De Trinitate* Augustine has been concerned with the individual's search for God within its own soul. There has been a minimal reference to human obligations in a spiritual sense as social beings. This aspect of Augustine's teaching is partly revealed in the *Discourses on the Psalms*. In particular, as Abbot Butler has noted, it receives fuller treatment in the exegesis of Psalm XLI.[99] Even here, however, it takes second place to extirpation of sin within the individual soul. Psalm XLI exemplifies Augustine's approach to exegesis and of course represents a very small fraction of his exegetical works. However, it must suffice in the compass of this study as exemplifying the poetic strain in his spirituality.

The Psalm, Augustine notes, is sung as a song of understanding: 'Like as the hart desireth the water-brooks, so longeth my soul after Thee, O God'.[100] He pursues the familiar theme, the search for God is the search for understanding: 'He is both the Fountain and the Light; for it is in Light that we shall see Light'[101] and: 'Everyone who hath understanding is enlightened by a certain light; not a corporeal, not a carnal one, not an outward, but an inward light'.[102]

To see this 'Light' the inward eye must be prepared, initially by the destruction of the serpents within: 'Long for the water-brooks; God hath wherewith to refresh thee and to satisfy thee when thou comest to Him, a-thirst, like the swift-footed hart, after the destruction of the serpents'.[103] The allusion is to the hart's capacity to kill serpents, after which its thirst is inflamed more violently. The serpents are the vices and passions which have to be controlled. The initial step in the ascent to God is to eliminate the distractions inherent in bodily nature.

In his exegesis, Augustine then begins a search for God in the way now familiar, within the soul. His quest takes him above the soul:

> His dwelling place is above my soul, from thence He beholds me; from thence He governs me and provides for me; from thence He appears to me and calls me, and directs me; leads me in the way, and to the end of my way.[104]

God also has a 'tabernacle' on earth, the Church, where He can be sought:

> God's tabernacle on earth is the Faithful. How much is there I admire in this tabernacle: – the self-conquest and the virtues of God's servants. I admire the

---

[99] Butler, *Western mysticism*, 21-24. The quotations from *Discourses on the Psalms* cited below are from Butler, based on a condensed text. See fn. 7 above. In his text Butler refers to Psalm XLI but his source refers to it as XLII.

[100] St Augustine, *Discourses on the Psalms* XLII, 2.

[101] *Ibid.*

[102] *Ibid.*

[103] *Ibid.*, XLII, 3.

[104] *Ibid.*, XLII, 8.

presence of those virtues in the soul; but still I am walking in the place of the tabernacle. I pass beyond these also; and admirable though the tabernacle be, yet when I come to the house of God, I am struck dumb with astonishment.[105]

The idea that God can be found in His faithful servants within the Church is, as Abbot Butler remarks, 'a unique, but surely a striking and fruitful, conception. For the individual soul, the example of others provides a "final lift up to the mystic height"'.[106] As is made clear, however, most of the effort in attaining the mystic experience of the vision of God was to be made by the individual cooperating with grace; the Christian community provides encouragement. The example of the Saints reinforces faith and gives hope; it encourages the faithful to live the life of charity and humility. This emphasis on the individual soul's relation with God also emphasises the tension implicit in his thought between the active and contemplative lives. The call of the active life is by no means neglected but in Augustine's spiritual thought it seems to run a struggling second. It is a matter of priorities perhaps. Root out evil and return to God; all else follows.

Reflection

Prior to his return to the Christian faith, Augustine had been much impressed by the writings of the Neoplatonists and particularly Plotinus. He is generous in his acknowledgments of his debt. It is not surprising then that his post-conversion vision of God perpetuates some key attributes of the Neoplatonic 'One'.

The attribute of God as 'unchangeable' is fundamental to his vision. The mutability of the corporeal world suggests a source which is unchangeable, to which the human spirit longs to return. Happiness can only be found in that which is not subject to change. It is the desire for happiness and the recognition of the source of it in an unchangeable essence which provides the motivation for the ascent to God.

Closely linked with the attribute of immutability is that of beauty. It was, as Henry has pointed out, the feeling for beauty in Plotinus that helped to attract Augustine.[107] The 'beauty of God' so ancient and so fresh is a constant theme of Augustine's as Rowan Williams has pointed out.[108] If you can conceive anything more beautiful than God, so much the worse for your efforts at love.[109] And, 'If creation is beautiful how much more lovely its Creator must be'.[110]

---

[105] *Ibid.*, XLII, 9.
[106] Butler, *Western mysticism*, 25.
[107] P. Henry, *La vision d'Ostie: Sa place dans la vie et l'oeuvre de saint Augustin*, Paris 1938, 77.
[108] Rowan Williams, *Wound of knowledge*, London: Darton, Longman & Todd, 1981, 74.
[109] *Ibid.*, quoted from *In Ps.*,43,16.
[110] *Ibid.*, 75, quoted from *In Ps.*, 39,8. See also *Ps.*,79,14; *Ps.*,84.9; *Ps.*85,9.

Partly Neoplatonic and partly Johannine are the attributes of 'Truth' and 'Light'[111] which are linked with the concept of God as ultimate reality – 'ad id quod est'.[112] The Christian influences expand this concept but there always remains the element of mystery in Augustine's concept which underlies his thinking the *'semper est…incommutabiliter manet quod Deus est'.*[113]

It has also been noticed that Augustine's descriptions of the final ascent to God and the direct experience of Him, particularly in the description of the vision of Ostia in the *Confessions*, are closely linked with Plotinian images and concepts. However, once again, the emphasis on personal experience in Augustine's account is something that is missing from the Neoplatonists and the Greek Fathers whose descriptions are more objective.[114] However, it is important to recognise the way in which Augustine's formulation of the concept of God and his attributes are framed in the ideas drawn from the Neoplatonist inheritance and how these ideas become part of the Christian frame of reference.

However, it would be wrong to emphasise too greatly the influence of Neoplatonic ideas in Augustine's concept of God. The Christian ideas clearly predominate. Augustine's God is a God of love who cares for his creation. He is principally a 'Creator' whose very act of creation *ex nihilo* is an act of love. This contrasts decisively with the Neoplatonic notion of the 'One', 'of whom nothing can be said'.[115] Furthermore, Augustine's unique development of the God who has revealed himself as 'Trinity', dominates his ideas. God the Father has some attributes of the Neoplatonic 'One' but even here the notion of 'Creator' is uniquely Judaeo-Christian.[116] When it comes to God as 'Mediator', 'Saviour' and 'The Word' as he is revealed in Christ, Augustine has moved out of the Neoplatonic world altogether. And likewise in the third person of the Holy Trinity, there is little resemblance between Neoplatonic concepts of 'emanation and return' and Augustine's Christian inheritance. The Holy Spirit is God as 'Love';

---

[111] St Augustine, *Confessions*, VII, 10, 16: 'Not this ordinary light which all flesh may look upon, not as it were a greater of the same kind, as though the brightness of this should be manifold brighter and with its greatness take up all space. Not such was this Light, but other, yea, far other from all else. Nor was it above my soul, as oil above water, nor yet as heaven above earth; but higher than my soul, because it made me; and I believe It, because I was made by It. He that knows the Truth knows what Light is; and He that knows It, knows Eternity. Love knoweth It. O eternal Truth, and true Love, and lovable Eternity Thou art my God, to Thee do I sigh day and night'.

[112] *Ibid.*, VII,17, 23.

[113] St Augustine, *Discourses on the Psalms*, CXXV, 8.

[114] Louis Bouyer, *A history of Christian spirituality*, vol.I: *The spirituality of the New Testament fathers*, (tr. Mary P. Ryan) London: Burns & Oates, 1982, 493, 494.

[115] Louth, 'Origins', 38, and Coppleston, *History of philosophy*, vol. 1 part 2, 210, 211.

[116] Coppleston, *History of philosophy*, vol. 1 part 2, 209. 'Goodness may be attributed to the 'One' provided it is not attributed as an inhering quality'.

it is the very antithesis of the Neoplatonists' 'One' whose emanations proceed out of 'necessity'.[117]

It is of course in the notions of God as 'Trinity' and 'Love' that Augustine's spirituality is rooted. Although Augustine is fundamentally influenced by the Platonic notion of the human as a spiritual being, of the human being as 'spirit in a body' that gives primacy to the spiritual ahead of the corporeal, the Christian inheritance nevertheless clothes the Neoplatonic notions in a distinctive Christian cloth. Humans are made 'after the image and in the likeness' of God. It is through this gift of creation that they come to participate in God. They are not, as the Neoplatonists believe, assimilated by the Godhead. They are of separate substance from God though shaped in the Trinitarian image of God; that image gives rise to the celebrated analogy between Father, Son and Holy Spirit and the soul with its attributes of memory, understanding and will. God in the shape of the Holy Spirit dwells within them and may transform their wills into an unquenchable desire for God which we know as 'love' – a love whose characteristic is its complete devotion to doing God's will.[118]

The major difference between Augustine's vision of humanity and the Neoplatonist concept is the doctrine of the 'Fall'. The 'Fall' is seen by Augustine as humanity's turning away from the common and universal good to seeking a private good. In this turning away from God's will they have irreparably damaged their relation with God which can only be restored by God's free gift of His pardon and grace. The importance of Christ as 'Mediator' and 'Saviour' is, of course, central to this idea of the relationship between God and humanity, through which the image of God in humans is gradually restored to a 'likeness' of God. Christ both shows the way in which humans can be restored as 'the Word made Flesh' and also gave humans the means to save themselves through His death on the cross. In Augustine's vision of humanity there is ambivalence. On the one hand humans are corrupt, fallen, tossed about by the whims of the body and essentially helpless without God's grace. On the other, they have this great gift that they have been made in the 'image and likeness' of God and, as the recipients of God's love, have the capacity to become as 'children' of God. Augustine

---

[117] *Ibid.*, 210, 211.

[118] St Augustine, *De civitate Dei*, vol. II, bk. XIV, chap. vii, 33: 'For he, that is resolved to love God and his neighbour according unto God and not man, is for this love called a man of good will; and this is called more commonly "charity" in the Scriptures, though sometimes it be called love therein also (…) This I thought worth recital, but some say *dilectio*, charity is one thing, and *amor* love, another; and that the first is used in the good, and the latter in the bad sense (…) But we wished to show that our Scriptures which we place far above their authorities, do not use *amor* and *dilectio* with any such distinct difference (…) Love then desiring to enjoy what it loves is desire; and enjoying it is joy; flying what it hates, it is fear; feeling it, it is sorrow'. Notice here also the antithesis between 'joy' and 'sorrow'.

is aware both of humanity's fallen nature and of their supernatural destiny. He has developed both aspects. It is in his vision of human being which he has brought to life in an unsurpassed way by the profundity of his self reflection, that Augustine's unique contribution to spirituality is expressed. He has brought together the Platonic concept of the primacy of the spirit in human beings, with the idea of the 'Fall' and their destiny to be restored to a 'likeness' of God. This concept of humanity colours the relationship between God and human beings in a uniquely Augustinian way and gives his spirituality, his idea of the ascent to God, a tension, a sense of ebb and flow, of 'highs' and 'lows' which is its characteristic; the high points of rapture, joy, lyrical beauty and the low points of self deprecation, a sense of unworthiness, and a devaluation of the human body. Like Augustine himself his spirituality is passionate. Rowan Williams has aptly called it 'the Clamour of Heart'.[119]

However, this aspect of his spirituality, important though it is, should not be allowed to obscure the other aspect, his 'intellectualism'. Abbot Butler recognises that the process by which the soul mounts up to contemplation is 'for the most part intellectual in idea and in language, sometimes frankly Plotinian'. He goes on:

> Western mystics commonly represent contemplation as attained to by, and in absorption in, prayer; but for Augustine it seems to have been primarily an intellectual process – informed indeed by intense religious warmth, but still primarily intellectual. It is the search for something not subject to change, that leads the soul up to God and it is represented as a great effort of intellect and will. In culmination the experience is identical in kind with those described by later mystics.[120]

It is by the intellect, of course, that Augustine seeks to confirm what he accepts by faith; *Credo ut intellegam*. It is in the application of intellect that a fuller understanding of faith is developed. But grace and faith always precede. It is not by intellect that fallen humanity attains to the threshold of the ascent to God, it is by grace. And indeed throughout the 'ascent', through 'purification' and 'recollection' and in 'contemplation', there is an interaction between the intellect and grace; by intellect recognising and responding to love. In most of Augustine's

---

[119] Williams, *Wound of knowledge*, 68-69.
[120] Butler, *Western mysticism*, 34. Cf. also John Burnaby's comment in *Amor Dei*, London: Hodder & Stoughton, 1938, 65: 'The form of this "inchoate contemplation" is that very "search" for God of which so many of Augustine's writings, and above all, the second parts of the *Confessions* and the *De Trinitate* provide examples. The method has been well described by the Augustinian Father Fulbert Cayré (*La contemplation Augustienne* , 240). It is "through an intellectual discipline, mystical in tendency, to lift the reader, little by little, to that spiritual state which is the indispensable condition of the fuller enlightenment". The aim is not to demonstrate theological propositions, but to show God, to bring Him into the heart, so that He may be "felt"'.

writings the pursuit of understanding is part of prayer. Prayers of petition and praise are interwoven into the fabric of his philosophising. The *Confessions* are above all a personal *Te Deum*.

CHAPTER II

ST GREGORY THE GREAT

The Pastoral Transvaluation of Augustinian Spirituality

St Augustine combined the speculative and emotional aspects of religion 'in a measure perhaps not achieved by any other'. St Gregory is the almost perfect complement; a man of most powerful practical intelligence who combined the provision of solutions to the pressing problems of the needs of Church and community with a balanced view of the contemplative and active aspects of the individual Christian life.[1] Together they provided a most powerful interpretation and example to the mediaeval Church of scriptural and patristic teaching. The more so since Gregory, the great preacher, simplified and popularised Augustine's teaching, harmonising a most cogent and all-embracing intellectual system with a practical rule of life.[2]

The purpose of this discussion is to show how St Augustine's language and cognitive framework was adopted and transvalued by St Gregory to meet the pastoral needs of the Church of his times. It is not known whether Gregory was acquainted with Augustine's *Confessions* prior to his own conversion. Very little is known about the circumstances surrounding it other than its life-changing impact. In the prefatory letter to the *Morals on Job* he looks back on the experience:

> I explained how I had put off the grace of conversion for such a long time. Even after I was filled with heavenly desire, I preferred to be clothed in secular garb. What I ought to seek in relation to the love of eternity had already been revealed to me, but long-standing habit so bound me that I could not change my outward

---

[1] Butler, *Western mysticism*, 206 and 176.

[2] F. Homes Dudden, *Gregory the Great: His place in history and thought*, London:Longman, Green and Co., 1905, vol.2, 285 and 442. R.A.Markus in the Preface of *Gregory the Great and his world* (Cambridge: Cambridge University Press, 1997), in which he seeks to update Dudden's work in the light of subsequent research (see his bibliography), comments: 'His book remains the classic account, at any rate in English (...) Books I and II remain the best narrative history available of Gregory's Pontificate'. Evidence of Gregory's influence in the Middle Ages has been collected by H. de Lubac, *Exégèse médiévale*, Paris 1959, 538-548: 'Le moyen âge grégorien'.

life (…) Finally I fled all this with anxiety (sollicite) and sought the safe haven of the monastery.[3]

Sollicite in this context suggests, perhaps, that a frighteningly inexplicable resolution of emotional tension marked the 'turning' point which enabled him to take the final step. There can be little doubt from the evidence of the echoes in his language that Gregory would have pondered Augustine's experience in the contemplative phase of his post-conversion period. Augustine had abandoned the prospect of marriage and a successful career, which might have led to a provincial governorship, to concentrate on the meaning of the divine love that had been shown to him in such dramatic manner as recounted in the *Confessions*. An analogous experience of divine love infusing his life may have triggered Gregory's response in which he turned his home into a monastery and established six other foundations with the balance of his wealth. In doing so he abandoned a career that had taken him at the age of thirty-three to the office of Prefect of Rome, the highest administrative post in the city. His experience of divine love perhaps provided him with independent confirmation of the power behind Augustine's transformation and of the cogency of the teaching that flowed from it. Not surprisingly, therefore, the Augustinian framework became the foundation of his teaching.[4] Nevertheless the circumstances of his ministry and the challenges he faced were different from those Augustine had encountered at the beginning of the fifth century. His work and great achievements after he became Bishop of Rome in 590, in ecclesiastical organisation, statesmanship and missionary initiatives, are well known.[5] In this discussion we shall neglect them, important as they are in Church history, to concentrate upon the manner in which he interpreted the call of divine love, for it is here that he provided the powerful complement to Augustine's spiritual teaching which was carried forward into the spirituality of the mediaeval Church.

The concepts of 'love' and 'charity' are central to both Gregory's and Augustine's teaching about the relationship between the individual and God and consequently, of that between individuals. However Gregory is not so much interested in a metaphysical explanation of either concept, nor therefore in the antithesis between love and knowledge. To appreciate how Gregory transvalues these concepts it is necessary to go to his writings and the context in which they were produced.

---

[3] Quoted by Bernard McGinn, *The growth of mysticism*, vol. II of *The presence of God: A history of Western Christian mysticism*, New York: The Crossroad Publishing Company, 1994, 34 and 432 fn.2 for the Latin text and the source.

[4] Markus, *Gregory the Great and his world*, 40, '…in all essentials it was Augustine's conceptual structures that shaped the world of his imagination'.

[5] For an excellent overview see Margaret Deanesly, *A history of the mediaeval church 590-1500*, London: Methuen, 1981, 15-28.

We will therefore follow the thematic development of his thought through their several stages that correspond broadly with his experience in his post-conversion career. He spent five years as a monk before being called upon to serve as a regional Deacon in Rome. He was then appointed to Constantinople as papal nuncio. A number of his monks joined his household there and the *Morals on Job* were written for their edification. His other major works were written after his appointment as Bishop of Rome.[6] It is not surprising that the relationship between the active and contemplative lives should preoccupy him and this is where we shall begin. That discussion will lead into a consideration of the significance of 'contemplation' and 'the vision of God' which appear like leitmotivs in his teaching. Finally, we will discuss the distinction he draws between the concepts, first of 'love', and then of 'charity', for it is here that the core of the transvaluation process from Augustine's to his own teaching is primarily evident.

The Two Lives

St Gregory provides the classic definitions of the two lives:

> The contemplative life is: to retain indeed with all one's mind the love of God and neighbour but to rest from exterior action, and cleave only to the desire of the Maker, that the mind may now take no pleasure in doing anything, but having spurned all cares, may be aglow to see the face of its Creator; so that it already knows how to bear with sorrow the burden of the corruptible flesh and with all its desires to seek to join the hymn-singing choirs of angels, to mingle with the heavenly citizens and to rejoice in its everlasting incorruption in the sight of God.[7]

The purpose of withdrawal from the world is to concentrate the mind on the love of God and neighbour and thus come to see God face to face. The concomitants of such a life are asceticism and praise; asceticism because of sorrow; praise because of joy.

---

6 Dom Jean Leclercq in *The spirituality of the Middle Ages* as vol. 2 in *A history of Christian spirituality*, New York: Seabury Press, 1982, 6. The works from this period cited in this chapter are *Homilies on Ezekial, Homilies on the Gospels,* the four books of *Dialogues* and the *Pastoral Care.* Editions are cited in the appropriate footnotes. See chap. 1 for Leclercq's penetrating overview of Gregory's teaching and significance.

7 Gregory the Great, *Homilies on Ezekiel,* ii,ii,8 [abbreviated to *Ezekiel* in the notes which follow] is quoted by Butler in *Western mysticism,* 246ff. The Latin source referred to for all quotations from *Homilies on Ezekiel* is *Corpus Chistianorum: Series latina,* cxlii, Gregorius Magnus, *Homiliae in Hiezechihilem prophetam* (Turnholti 1971). The Homilies on Ezekiel were preached to mixed audiences in the Lateran basilica after Gregory became Pope in 590. The two quotations which follow are from the same source.

The active life he defines, with a characteristic Roman practicality, as follows:

> …to give bread to the hungry, to teach the ignorant the word of wisdom, to correct the erring, to recall to the path of humility our neighbour when he waxes proud, to tend the sick, to dispense to all what they need and to provide those entrusted to us with the means of subsistence'.

It is a *manifesto* of good works.

The relationship between the two lives is then developed:

> While placed in this life we taste only the beginnings of intimate contemplation; whereas the active life can be fully laid hold of. Wherefore the active life ceases with this present world; but the contemplative life begins here, that it may be perfected in the heavenly country, because the fire of love which begins to burn here, when it sees Him whom it loves, will in His love blaze up the more. Therefore the contemplative life is by no means taken away, for when the light of the present world is withdrawn it is perfected.

He illustrates the relationship with the story of Lia and Rachel, the two wives of Jacob, – as indeed Augustine had:[8]

> Rachel was beautiful but sterile because the contemplative life is lovely in the mind, but while it longs to rest in silence, it does not generate sons by preaching; it sees but brings not forth, because while it loves the pursuit of its quiet, it is less inflamed in gathering others; and what it sees within it is unable to open out to others by preaching. Lia, on the other hand, was dim-eyed but fruitful; because the active life, while occupied in work, sees less; but while now by word, now by example, it incites others to imitate itself, it generates many children in its good work. And it is not able to stretch the mind in contemplation, yet from the fact that it acts exteriorly, it is able to beget followers. The active life is lived first, that afterwards the contemplative may be attained to.[9]

The objective of the active life is to bring others to the love of God:

> So usually it is useful for the mind to turn back from the contemplative to the active, that by the very fact that the contemplative has inflamed the mind, the active may be more perfectly held.[10]

St Augustine had said that the contemplative life had a productiveness of its own, 'it is aflame with the love of generating for it desires to teach what it knows'.[11] Gregory echoes the thought:

---

8   Augustine, *Contra Faustum*, xxii, 52 quoted by Butler, *Western mysticism*, 230.
9   *Ezekiel*, ii,ii,10.
10 *Ibid.*, ii,ii,11.
11 Augustine, *Contra Faustum*, xxii, 54 quoted by Butler, *Western mysticism*, 252.

Holy men when they soar aloft to the contemplation of things on high, when they bind the first fruits of their spirit in the love of the heavenly country, but weighed down by the load of human life, return to themselves, they declare unto their brethren the heavenly goods they were able to contemplate at any rate in a mirror, and influence their minds with the love of that inward brightness which they are neither to see as it is, nor utter as they saw it; but while they speak their words pierce and set on fire the hearts of those that hear.[12]

There is a necessity to pass on to others what one has been privileged to receive:

[W]hoever reaps benefit by seeing spiritual things is bound by speaking to lay them before others. For he sees in order that he may announce, by the fact that he reaps benefit for himself, by preaching has a care also for the advance of his neighbour.

The interaction between contemplation and good works, particularly preaching, is at the heart of Gregory's spirituality. He seems, through his public career, to have gained a considerable knowledge of people and acquired a sensitivity to their differing needs. In the *Pastoral Care* he describes no less than thirty-five types of people for whom the preacher must tailor the matter and delivery.[13] He makes the point in another context that 'the compositions of souls are infinitely varied one with another',[14] some suited to the active life and some to the contemplative but 'the active life is the lot of many, the contemplative of few'.[15] For the spiritually minded the active life alone is unsatisfactory:

Whosoever already looks down upon all earthly objects of desire, whosoever spreads himself out in the labours of an active life, finds that it by no means suffices him to do great things without, unless by contemplation he also have power to penetrate into interior mysteries.[16]

---

[12] Ezekiel, i,v,13 and ii,ii,4 below.

[13] Dudden, *Gregory the Great*, vol.1, 236. *Liber regulae pastoralis*, translated as *Pastoral care* by H.S. Bramley (London: Parker & Co., 1874). Latin source is from *Patrologia cursus completus, Series latina*, (ed. J.P. Migne) Paris 1844-1864, Vol. 77, 13-128 (henceforth abbreviated as PL, followed by the volume number).

[14] Gregory the Great, *Morals on Job*, vi, 57 quoted by Butler, *Western mysticism*, 272. 'Sed inter haec magnopere sciendum est quia valde inter se diversae sunt conspersiones animorum'. The Latin source for the *Morals* referred to is *Corpus Christianorum, series latina* (Turnhout: Brepols, 1955ff), cxliii, *Moralia in Job libri i-x*. The other books of the *Morals* appear in *Corpus Christianorum* as follows; cxliiia libri xi-xxii (1979) and cxliiib libri xxiii-xxxv (1985). The *Morals* were preached to the monks who accompanied Gregory on his posting to Constantinople as the Pope's Apocrisiarius or nuncio in the period 579-585. *Morals on Job* has been abbreviated to *Morals*.

[15] *Ibid.*, *Morals*, xxxii, 4, 'quia activa vita multorum est, contemplativa paucorum'.

[16] *Ibid.*, vi,55, 'sed quisquis jam terena desideria despicit, quisquis se per activa vitae opera extendit, nequaquam ei sufficit magna exterius agere, nisi etiam per contemplationem valeat interna penetrare'.

This latter passage from the *Morals* may well be one of the keys to Gregory's own decision to abandon public life, use all his means to endow monasteries and to become a monk himself. Later the needs of the Church and community were to persuade him to return to the active life, first as Deacon, then as papal diplomat, abbot and finally Pope.[17] Nevertheless, the need to regroup spiritual resources in the practice of contemplation seems to have been present in all phases of his active ministry. Like all those so energetically engaged in the 'active' life, for example St Augustine before him and St Bernard and William of St Thierry after him, Gregory longs for some respite from the continual demands of high office, for the quiet which alone enables the contemplative to put aside the distractions of the world and concentrate the mind to move into the spiritual dimension.

Contemplation

What is it that motivates the Christian either to the contemplative or active life? For it is clear that Gregory regards not only the active but also the contemplative life as open to all: 'It is not the case that the grace of contemplation is given to the highest and not given to the lowest',[18] and 'We see daily in Holy Church that very many, while they manage well external things that come to them, are by the grace given them led moreover to mystic intelligence; so that they faithfully administer outward things and are gifted greatly with inward understanding'.[19]

In both contexts he emphasises that grace, a gift freely given by God, is the key; but it is a gift that has to be desired; and desire springs from faith. For Gregory the role of the preacher is of great importance as a catalyst in generating faith. He may have had in mind the role of St Ambrose in Augustine's conversion. In speaking of the role of the preacher and religious superior, he says:

> [I]t behoves the good ruler to desire to please men, but so as to draw their neighbour by the sweetness of their character to a fondness for Truth; not that they should desire to be loved themselves, but that they make the affection borne to them, as it were, a sort of road by which they may lead the hearts of their hearers to the love of their Creator. For it is hard for a preacher who is not loved, however right may be his warnings, to be heard gladly.[20]

---

[17] For Gregory's life prior to his pontificate see Dudden, vol.1 and for his pontificate, vol.2.

[18] *Ezekiel*, ii,v,19.

[19] Gregory the Great, *Homilies on the Gospels*, ix, 5 [Abbreviated to *Homilies* in the notes which follow] quoted by Butler, *Western mysticism*, 186, 271. Latin source PL 76, 1075-1312. They were preached in the Lateran basilica post 591. *Intellectus mysticus*, the use of the word 'mystical' in its later sense is noteworthy.

[20] Gregory the Great, *Pastoral care*, ii,8. Quoted by Dudden, *Gregory the Great*.

and

> The speech, therefore, of teachers ought to be fashioned according to the condition of the hearers, that it may both be suited to each of their own needs and yet may never depart from the system of general edification (…) whence also every teacher, to the end that he may edify all in the one virtue of charity, ought to touch the hearts of his hearers out of one system of teaching but not with one and the same address.[21]

And moving back to the theme that the preacher must be prepared to teach both wise and dull; of the wise, 'we must labour that they may become more wisely foolish, that they may abandon their foolish wisdom and learn the wise foolishness of God', and of the dull, 'that they pass over as from a nearer point, from that which is accounted folly to true wisdom'. As a physician of souls, Gregory regarded the cleric's main instrument as preaching. For Gregory, therefore, who pre-eminently regarded his role as that of teacher, contemplation, and its sweetness, was a reward but also a goad. It was the source of sweetness, illumination and of renewal:

> Sometimes the soul is admitted to some unwanted sweetness of interior relish [an echo of St Augustine] and is suddenly in some way refreshed when breathed on by the glowing spirit; and is the more eager the more it gains a taste of something to love. And it desires that within itself which it feels to taste sweet within, because it has in truth from the love of its sweetness, become vile in its own sight; after having been able in whatever way to enjoy it, it discovers what it has hitherto been without. It endeavours to cling closely to it, but is kept back from its strength by its own remaining weakness; and because it is unable to contemplate its purity it counts it sweet to weep, and sinking back to itself to strew the tears of its own weakness. For it cannot fix its mind's eye on that which it has with hasty glance seen within itself, because it is compelled by its own old habits to sink downwards. It meanwhile pants and struggles and endeavours to go above itself, but sinks back, overpowered with weariness, into its own familiar darkness. A soul thus affected has to endure itself as the cause of a stubborn contest against itself, and all this controversy about ourselves causes no small amount of pain, when we are engaged in it, whatever pleasure may be blended therewith.[22]

In Abbot Butler's view this and similar passages reflect St Gregory's own experience, though the images and sometimes the expressions are similar to those used by Augustine. Certainly the power of contemplation as a transforming experience is shared with St Augustine, who expresses it finely: 'There the sole and all-embracing virtue is to love what you see and the supreme happiness to possess

---

[21] *Ibid.*, iii, Prologue. The quotations which follow are from the same source.
[22] *Morals*, xxiii,43.

what you love'.[23] For St Gregory the attainment of contemplation is the culmination of a struggle, a striving and he uses the image of the wrestler with the
attainment of contemplation resembling the moments when the wrestler gets
on top of his opponent.[24] But 'love' is the engine of the contemplative process.[25]
Success is given only to those who love[26] and is a reflection of how much one
loves.[27]

The central place of love in the contemplative life is paralleled also in the
active life. Acts of piety without love are valueless: 'The love of God is never
otiose. If it exists it works great things; if it does not work it is not love'.[28]

Gregory does not ask, as St Augustine does, how can one love what one does
not know. He starts from the premise that God is love and that love grows as
one lives the *vita fidei* (life of faith).[29] However, Gregory's vision of God helps
to illuminate his idea of love which is perhaps more practical and less emotional
than St Augustine's.

The Vision of 'God'

Some of the ways in which Gregory refers to God or his manifestation in contemplation, have already been quoted: 'sweetness',[30] 'the taste of something to
love;'[31] 'glowing Spirit', 'purity'. A favourite image is 'unencompassed light which
is not yet seen in its brightness' but shines in the mind as if through a chink; or
'unencompassed spirit' who 'incomprehensibly governs what he has incomprehensibly created'.[32] How is man to fathom, he asks, the greatness of Him who
made the soul.

---

[23] Augustine, *De genesi ad litteram*, xxii, 26,54 (PL 34). 'Una ibi et tota virtus est amare quod
videas et summa felicitas habere quod amas'.

[24] *Ezekiel*, ii,ii,12.

[25] *Morals*, vi,58, 'machina quippe mentis est vis amoris quae hanc dum a mundo extrahit in astra
sustollit'.

[26] *Ezekiel*, ii,v,17.

[27] *Morals*, vi,58, 'unde necesse est ut quisquis ad contemplationis studia properat semet ipsum
prius subtiliter interroget, quantum amat'.

[28] *Homilies*, 30,32. Quoted by Dudden, *Gregory the Great*, vol. 2, 350.

[29] Dudden, *Gregory the Great*, 437.

[30] *Ezekiel*, ii,ii,13, 'dulcedo'.

[31] *Morals*, xx,iii,43, 'tantoque magis inhiat, quanto magis quod amet, degustat'.The phrases which
follow, 'ardenti spiritu', and 'et quia cuius munditiae contemplari non valet, flare dulce habet',
and viii,50, 'incircumscripti luminis' are from the same source.

[32] *Ezekiel*, ii,v,9, 'incircumscripto spiritu, incomprehensibiliter regit incomprehensibiliter
creavit'.

Gregory did not believe that it was possible to see God 'face to face' in this life.[33] Whenever he refers to God the vision is indistinct.[34] He stresses the unbounded nature of the image; it is 'unencompassed', 'incorporeal', a momentary glimpse[35] is captured or it is seen as a sunbeam seen through a chink; something of the inmost realities seen through a mist. In this life it is like seeing the sun through a fog or cloud.[36] Gregory comments on Psalm xvii.10 'caligo sub pedibus eius': 'By those beneath He is not seen in that brightness wherewith He exercises dominion among those above'.[37]

In another passage he refers to the experience as seen 'sub eiusdam caligine imaginationis', under the fog of some sort of imagining.

There is no *De Trinitate* from Gregory. The nearest he comes to a theological analysis is illustrated in the following passage from the *Morals*:

> Every man that apprehends something of the Eternal Being by contemplation, beholds the same through this co-eternal Image (...) when there His Eternity is perceived as far as the capability of our frail nature admits, His Image is set before the eyes of the mind, in that when we really strain towards the Father, as far as we receive Him we see Him by His image, i.e. His Son. And by that Image which was born of Himself without beginning, we strive in some sort to obtain a glimpse of Him who hath neither beginning nor ending.[38]

It is in Christ, that God has made himself known to man.

But the experience of God is nevertheless real:

> When the mind employed in prayer, pants after the form (species) of its Maker, burning with divine longings, it is united to that which is above, it is disjoined from that below; it opens itself in the affection of fervent passion, that it may take in, and while taking in, kindles itself; and whilst with longing desire, the soul is agape after heavenly objects, in a marvellous way it tastes the very thing it longs to get.[39]

---

[33] Note also *Ezekiel*, i,viii,30: The vision of the glory but of the likeness of the glory; that it may be shown that with whatever effort the human mind strains, even if it have repressed the phantasies of bodily images from its thought and have removed from the eyes of the heart all finite spirits, still while placed in mortal flesh it is not able to see the glory of God as it is. But whatever of it that is which shines in the mind, is a likeness and not itself.

[34] *Morals*, v,53, 'adhuc Deum in quasi in nocturna visione cernimus cum procul dubio sub incerta contemplatione caligamus' and xv,20, 'fluvius autem torrens est ipsa inundatio spiritus sancti quae in contemplantis animum exuberant, infusione colligitur cum mens plus quam intellegere sufficit, repletur...'.

[35] *Morals*, viii,50, 'quam videt raptim'.

[36] *Ibid.*, xviii,39. This is the basic image underpinning the remarkable fourteenth-century treatise *The cloud of unknowing*.

[37] *Ibid.*, xvii,39, 'caligo est namque ei sub pedibus quia non ea claritate ab inferioribus cernitur qua in superioribus dominator', and v,53.

[38] *Ibid.*, v,63,64.

[39] *Ibid.*, xv,53.

And:

> Falling back upon itself [from contemplation] the soul is drawn to Him with
> closer bonds of love, whose marvellous sweetness, being unable to bear, she has
> just tasted of under an indistinct vision.[40]

But such experiences defy the powers of utterance:

> Their minds are inflamed with the love of that interior brightness, which they are
> able 'neither to see as it is nor to utter as they see it.[41]

and again,

> [O]ften the mind of him that loves is filled with so great a gift of contemplation
> that it has power to see what it has not the power to utter. The inundation of the
> Holy Spirit in exuberant outpouring is gathered in the soul of one in contempla-
> tion, when his mind is full beyond what he is able to comprehend.[42]

If words cannot adequately express the experience, the memory of it is inefface-
able:

> Such a one returning to good works feeds on the memory of God's sweetness and
> is nourished by pious acts without, and holy desires within; and they strive always
> to utter the memory of it by recollecting it and speaking of it.[43]

The experience of it may also engender self-knowledge:

> The higher the elevation whereat the mind of man contemplates the things that
> are eternal, so much the more terror-struck at her temporal deeds, she shrinks with
> dread, in that she thoroughly discovers herself guilty in proportion as she sees
> herself to have been out of harmony with that light which shines in the midst of
> darkness above her; and then it happens that the mind being enlightened, enter-
> tains the greater fear, as it more clearly sees by how much it is at variance with
> the rule of Truth.[44]

God is also spoken of as 'Truth' and 'Wisdom'.[45] In a passage in the *Dialogues*
Gregory explains St Benedict's experience in contemplation in the following
terms:

---

[40] *Ibid.*

[41] *Ezekiel*,i,v,13, 'in amorem intimae claritatis accendunt'.

[42] *Morals*, xv,20.

[43] *Ezekiel*, i,v,12.

[44] *Morals*, v,53.

[45] See Butler, *Western mysticism*, 76: 'I do not find that St Gregory anywhere explicitly identifies
this Truth with God; but there can be no doubt that by the "Boundless Truth" ("incircumspecta
veritas", *Morals*, v,66) he means God Himself. And he does identify with God the "Eternal
Light" ("Lux aeterna, quae Deus est". *Morals*, xxv,ll; "Lumen verum, Creator videlicet noster".
Morals, xxv,9.) But there is no suggestion of Augustine's conceptions that all truth is perceived

To the soul that sees the Creator every created thing is narrow. For however little it be of the light of the Creator that it beholds, all that is created becomes to it small; because by the very light of inmost vision the bosom of the mind is enlarged, and it is so expanded in God that it is above the world. But the seer's soul itself becomes also above itself and when in the light of God it is rapt above itself, it is broadened out interiorly; and while raised aloft it looks downwards, it understands how small is that which in its lowly estate it could not understand.[46]

Such is the illumination of the mind that is brought about by touching 'Wisdom'; the world is seen through God's eyes and our neighbour, as it were, is also seen through God's eyes.

The production of the *Dialogues*, a mediaeval bestseller, was Gregory's attempt to convince the demoralised populace of Rome, who had experienced successively devastation, pillage and all the horrors of war[47] and also later, natural disasters – floods, famine and drought[48] – that God was present among them in a tangible way. He was working through his saints who were themselves Romans and Italians. The need for this reassurance, through miracles and the power of holy men and their relics, was something Gregory, for all his urbanity, understood well. He had suffered in his childhood with the people he was addressing. He understood the power and menace of superstition in calamitous situations. For him, therefore, the times did not call for a *De Trinitate* but rather a work of hagiography which showed God working in people's lives, and above all, being on the side of the orthodox.[49]

Love

The practise of the love of God and neighbour are the core of St Gregory's spirituality. His understanding and use of the terms *amor* (love), and *caritas* (charity), give his spirituality its individuality for they reflect his personal experience.[50]

---

in unchangeable Truth above the mind, and the light in which purely intellectual truths are seen is God Himself'. If this is so then the passage which follows from *the Dialogues* must come very close to Augustine's conception, at least as perceived in contemplation.

[46] Gregory the Great, *The dialogues*, (ed. Mittermüller, 1880), ii,35. Quoted by Butler, *Western mysticism*, 86.

[47] See Dudden, *Gregory the Great*, appendix: 545 Totila laid siege to Rome; 546 Goths take Rome; 547 Rome recovered by Belisarius; 549 Rome again taken by the Goths.

[48] 589 floods in Italy; 590 floods in Italy; 591 drought and famine in Italy.

[49] See Joan M. Petersen, *The Dialogues of Gregory the Great in their late antique cultural background*, Toronto: Pontifical Institute of Mediaeval Studies, 1984 (Studies and Texts 69), 54 and ch.4, 90 et seq. Also Peter Brown, 'Society, demons and the rise of Christianity from Late Antiquity into the Middle Ages', in: idem, *Religion and society in the age of St Augustine*, 119-146.

[50] Butler, *Western mysticism*, 75.

It is perhaps surprising, therefore, in a man who understood, and placed such importance on, human motivation and behaviour, that he did not provide a psychological analysis of the concept that was the key, as we have seen, to his religion; 'love' is the engine of the contemplative life[51] and good works are valueless without 'love'. For St Augustine the response of the individual to the love of God was the central puzzle of religion; it led to his development of the 'image' theology and his analysis of the Trinity was in part focussed on the light it shed on human psychology.[52] Gregory's preoccupation is with 'faith' and the life of faith; love is the outcome or manifestation of that life.[53] It could be said that Gregory wanted to teach 'faith', while Augustine, to teach love'. The particular preoccupations and emphases of the two saints flavour their 'spirituality' but not the substance of their faith.

Homes Dudden has emphasised in his work the key role of *fides* and *vita fidei* in Gregory's religion, he nevertheless seems to have underemphasised the role of love. Dudden regards Gregory as the typical Roman, steeped in legalism and with a great capacity for organisation. Gregory is said to have viewed religion from the standpoint of law and discipline; his ideas centred on guilt, merit, satisfaction and penance; retribution and merit are the conceptions which determine its form; God's dealings with man are seen as a series of legal transactions; Tertullian modified by Augustine's spiritual characteristics of faith, love and grace.[54]

His Roman genius for organisation is said to be exemplified in his doctrine of the Church and sacraments. Doctrine is associated with church government and faith is made synonymous with obedience. Man is saved by obedience, by complying with ecclesiastical regulations, by performing definite duties. God's grace is given through ordinances, rites and ceremonies. Ecclesiastical institutions are essential for salvation. 'In this circle', he says 'we can readily trace the thought of the Roman administrator who sought to govern the souls of men by contrivances analogous to those of politics'.[55]

This judgement seems to place too much emphasis on Gregory's administrative achievements and too little on the 'conversion', and Gregory's own desire to pursue the contemplative life. The experience which led to his retirement initially from public life is reflected in the *dictum*, 'We hear the words of God if we act upon them',[56] which is a constant refrain. He tells us: 'Throughout Scripture God speaks to us only for this purpose, that He may lead us to the love of

---

[51] *Morals*, vi,58, 'for the force of love is an engine of the soul, which while it draws it out of the world, lifts it on high'.
[52] L. Bouyer, *History of Christian spirituality*, London: Burns & Oates, 1982, 493.
[53] Dudden, *Gregory the Great*, vol.2, 437.
[54] *Ibid.*, vol.2, 291.
[55] *Ibid.*
[56] *Ezekiel*, i,x,20 and *Morals*, vi,12; xv,17; xxii,8,9.

Himself and our neighbour',[57] and it is the light of love alone – the double love of God and man – 'which illumines the shades of human dullness'.[58]

In the absence of an analysis of 'love' it is necessary to explore the contexts in which he uses both *amor* and (in the next section) *caritas*, to understand more fully how he conceived them.

'Love' for Gregory is an innate capacity. Its seat is, as with St Augustine, in the will. It is reflected in a desire for the world – worldly goods, worldly success – or for God. In either case the object of desire is happiness. During the span of Gregory's lifetime it is patently obvious that in the disturbed state of Western Europe and particularly Rome, worldly happiness was an illusion, at least ephemeral. In fact Gregory believed the end of the world was at hand, which gave his teaching its penitential emphasis.[59] The alternative source of happiness was love of God: 'The sweetness of contemplation is worthy of love exceedingly for it opens up heavenly things and hides bodily'.[60]

Love of God is a strenuous process. It requires asceticism, the subjugation of bodily desires and then good works. Finally, in contemplation its desires are in part rewarded. But to achieve contemplation the desire must be great: 'For contemplation a man must question how much he loves'[61] and 'Greatness of contemplation given only to those that love'.[62] It might appear that contemplation was the reward for merit. This is not so because its attainment is accompanied by sorrow, compunction, tears, 'sweet weeping' and the realisation that it is wholly unmerited.[63] The soul cannot bear the purity and drops away,[64] only to have its desire rekindled. The experience of contemplation reinforces the desire for repetition; 'the soul has gained a taste for something to love'.

---

[57] *Ezekiel* i,x,l4.

[58] *Morals*, vi,12: 'Tenebras hebetudinis illustrat oculis amoris'.

[59] Dudden, *Gregory the Great*, Preface fn.1 quotes F. Gregorovius, *Rome in the Middle Ages* (London: 8 vols., 1894-1902), vol.2, 70: 'The sixth century is one of the most memorable in history. In it mankind experienced the overthrow of a great and ancient civilisation and on this account believed that the end of the world had come. A thick cloud of barbarism, as it were, of dust arising from the crash, hung over the Roman Empire devastated throughout its length and breadth by the destroying angel, dealing pestilence and other ills. The world entered upon a turning-point in its development'.

[60] *Ezekiel*, ii,ii,13.

[61] *Morals*, vi,58.

[62] *Ezekiel*, ii,v,17, 'quae magnitudo contemplationis quia concedi non nisi amantibus potest'.

[63] *Ibid.*, ii,ii,1, 'atque animus, culparum suarum conscius, dum recognoscit, quod audierit, doloris se iaculo percutit, et compunctionis gladio transfigit, Ut nihil ei nisi flere libeat et fluentis fletuum maculas lavare suavi fletu'.

[64] *Morals*, xxiii,43, 'inter haec anhelat, aestuat, super se ire conatur, sed familiares tenebras suas victa fatigatione relabitur'.and 'tantoque magis inhiat, quanto magis quod amet, degustat'.

The experience of contemplation transforms human desire by the 'inundation of the Holy Spirit in exuberant outpouring'.[65] Gregory does not actually say that love is the 'Holy Spirit' working in the soul. The image of 'exuberant outpouring' suggests an overflowing of energy that powers action: 'This love which the Holy Spirit inspires in man is an active love'.

He goes out of his way to stress that love must be fruitful: 'Let there be love then but not enervating'.[66] and it must be unselfish: 'For love then wonderfully mounts to the heights when it mercifully draws itself to the lowliness of its neighbour; and in proportion as it kindly descends to what is weak does it mightily return to the heights',[67] a happy reference to the example of Christ in the incarnation, crucifixion and resurrection.

Love of God and neighbour are perhaps not equally important but they are certainly complementary:

> The love of their neighbour may not interfere with the love of God; nor again the love of God cast out, because it transcends, the love of their neighbours[68]

and again:

> Neither so delight in repose for the sake of the love of God, as to put aside the care and service of our neighbour; nor busying itself for the love of neighbour, be so wedded thereto that, entirely forsaking quiet, it extinguish in itself the fire of love of the most High.

Gregory seems to accept that his audience knows what love is. He is not interested in a theology of love. His interest is practical. Love of God and neighbour is central to his concepts of both the contemplative and active lives. Love begins in faith and grows by leading the life of faith.

Charity

Unlike the use of the term *caritas* (charity) by St Augustine, where it is often used synonymously with love, *amor* or *dilectio*, St Gregory uses it to describe a virtue as opposed to a force. *Caritas* is associated with care for and service of our neighbours, with good works in particular.

There are a number of references to *caritas* as 'care':

---

[65] *Ibid.*, xv,20.

[66] *Pastoral care*, ii,6.

[67] *Ibid.*, ii,5.

[68] *Morals*, xxviii,33, 'quatenus nec amorem Dei praepediat amor proximi, nec amorem proximi, quia transcendet, abiciat amor Dei'.and vi,56.

For he sees in order that he may announce, who, by the fact that he reaps bene-fit for himself, by preaching has a care also for the advance also of his neighbour[69]

and

For by contemplation they rise into the love of God, but by preaching they return back to the service of their neighbour (...) In the sight of the eternal judge our charity should be coloured with the love both of God and of our neighbour that the converted soul may neither so delight in repose for the sake of the love of God, as to put aside the care and service of our neighbour.[70]

In this reference 'charity' is a virtue that gives 'colour' to life to the extent that it is informed by love of God and neighbour. It is the virtue of care and service for neighbour.

He is particularly concerned that charitable behaviour should be motivated only by love of God and neighbour: 'There are two commands of charity, the love of God and of our neighbour'.[71] There is a need for 'love' to be continu-ously rekindled: 'For they would freeze too speedily amid their outward works, good though they be, did they not constantly return with anxious earnestness to the fire of contemplation',[72] and 'they grow cold in inward love'.[73]

In the *Morals* he refers to what has been translated as: 'Lend themselves with the condescension of charity to the earthly necessities of others'.[74] This transla-tion is used by Abbot Butler, but it would seem 'condescensione' would be bet-ter rendered by 'humility' in this context. He commends in a passage from the *Pastoral Care*, the example of St Paul:

Who could search out the secrets of the third heaven, and yet condescend (hum-ble himself) to lay down rules for the regulation of the intercourse of carnal per-sons, being joined at once to the highest and the lowest by the bond of charity.[75]

In this context 'charity' seems to be used synonymously with 'love'. But in the prologue of the third book of the *Pastoral Care* he reverts to using it in the other sense: 'Whence also every teacher to the end that he may edify all in the one virtue of charity'.

---

[69] *Ezekiel*, ii,ii,4. (See also *Morals*, xxviii,33). 'Videt quippe ut annuntiet, qui in ea quod in se proficit etiam de profectu proximi praedicando curam gerit'.

[70] *Morals*, vi,56, 'caritas nostra Dei et proximi dilectione coloretur'.

[71] *Pastoral care*, i,7.

[72] *Morals*, xxx,8, 'citius enim in ipsa licet bona, exteriora opera frigescerent, nisi intentione sol-licita ad contemplationis ignem in cessanter redirent'.

[73] *Pastoral care*, ii,7.

[74] *Morals*, xix,45.

[75] *Pastoral care*, ii,5 and iii, Prologue.

It certainly seems that Gregory intends to use 'charity' to mean the virtue of good works informed by love, or perhaps the habitual activity of loving in contrast to its sacrificial inspiration in contemplation.

Reflection

The operative themes of St Gregory's spirituality are love of God and love of neighbour. The practice of love gives rise to the virtue of charity, which in almost all cases means doing 'good works'. Without love of neighbour there is no real love of God, for love of God is active; where love of God really exists, it is accompanied by the desire, the necessity, to introduce others to the ultimate joy.

Gregory recognises degrees of love, both of God and neighbour. It is evident in his teaching that love grows with the practice of contemplation and while it is recognised that perfection is unattainable in this life, perfection is nevertheless the goal. Perfection is attained when the soul can dwell forever in the full vision of God; when he is seen face to face. In this life Christians obtain only a glimpse of what beatitude means, but it is sufficient to enable them to understand 'perfection' and their own 'imperfection' and to generate a desire to be worthy of the sight of God for eternity.

What is true for the individual soul is true also for the Christian community, the Church. It has to be worthy of its calling as the body of Christ. Love of neighbour, then, recognises that Christians should be one with Christ. Neighbour must be loved as self for the love of God.

For Gregory, to live as a Christian was the basic challenge. He was quite capable of speculative thought, of absorbing, for example, Augustine's speculative theology, but his primary interest lay in teaching those in his care how to live as Christians and ultimately to attain the beatitude promised to all who follow Christ.

Gregory's teaching balances carefully the roles of the contemplative and active aspects of the Christian life. The two lives complement each other. If the pastoral emphasis in his teaching seems to predominate, it is, perhaps, because he believed the active life was the lot of the many.

There does not seem to be a great deal of justification for Homes Dudden's judgement about his teaching:

> His conception of religion, perhaps, was somewhat hard and unlovely. There was too much of the judgement, of tears and penance, of the fancies of the cloister. It lacked breadth and sunshine (...) He believed that Christ called on him to make his life a fiery martyrdom; and a fiery martyrdom in very truth his life was made.[76]

---

[76] Dudden, *Gregory the Great*, vol.2, 280 compared with Butler, *Western mysticism*, 171.

He seems to have missed, or discounted, the mystical basis of Gregory's religion which Abbot Butler has documented so fully. Both St Augustine and St Gregory believed that Christ's example was that of self-sacrifice. It was self-sacrifice rooted in great love. The Passion was 'hard and unlovely'. For the most part Christian life requires sacrifice, self-discipline, and asceticism; but not for their own sake. These characteristics only become exemplary and inspirational if they are founded in love. Both Augustine and Gregory found the source of Christian love in the mystical insights of contemplation and the grace that inspired them. The 'ebb and flow' of joy and sorrow in St Augustine's spirituality is a characteristic ambiance. There is perhaps more of the sorrow than the joy in St Gregory's; this may have led to Homes Dudden's judgement that his religion lacked 'sunshine', despite Gregory's emphasis on the primacy of love.

The explanation for the very real tension between joy and sorrow in Gregory's teaching perhaps lies in his experience. He had been baptised and brought up in a Christian home environment. Little is known of the interaction between Gregory's Christian background and the appalling circumstances of the siege and fall of Rome on two occasions before Gregory was ten years old. His family survived the hardships of these times with its wealth intact when many aristocratic families of similar background were impoverished.[77] The Roman university, where he was educated, had suffered from the withdrawal of Imperial funding. Its most celebrated teachers had departed.[78] Gregory's highly successful career as an administrator which took him to the most senior position in Rome by the age of thirty-three, was concerned with a city on the brink of ruin whose former glories were everywhere evident.[79] It is not difficult to understand how in these circumstances Gregory expounded the apocalyptic tradition of earlier periods and believed that the end of the world was at hand. It gave urgency to the task of Christian renewal as preparation for the Judgement.

The convictions that led him to give up his career at its peak and to give away his family wealth are not known with certainty.[80] Nevertheless, the path his life took from that time suggests a 'conversion' analogous to that of St Augustine. Not analogous, perhaps, to the extent of a moment of revelation in the garden which, for Augustine, put a long period of reflection into perspective, but a somewhat similar development of emotional tension culminating in an inexplicable cathartic experience of release, or of freedom. There seems to have been an empathy between Gregory and Augustine, however to be explained. We have suggested it might have found its inspiration in a common experience of

---

[77] Dudden, *Gregory the Great*, vol.1, ch.2.
[78] *Ibid.*, vol.1, ch.4.
[79] *Ibid.*, vol.1, ch.5.
[80] *Ibid.*, vol.1, ch.5 for a discussion of St Gregory's conversion.

'conversion', for Gregory absorbed Augustine's teaching to a remarkable degree. Homes Dudden, somewhat disparagingly by contrast with Butler, can say:

> Sufficient to remark that Gregory while adopting Augustinianism, to some extent debased it. He retained its superficial form without its profound meaning. He toned it down, mutilating it on certain sides and adapting it to vulgar intelligences. The Augustinianism which Gregory passed over to the Middle Ages does not represent the true Augustine.[81]

But Dudden also accepts that Gregory's interpretation still reflects the spiritual characteristics of Augustine's teaching on faith, love and grace.[82] Those are in fact the cornerstones of Gregory's own spiritual teaching.

G.R. Evans in her book on St Gregory's thought suggests that the art of the simplifier and populariser, like that of the caricaturist, is a very skilled one; it requires that one absorbs the essential characteristics and reproduces them with economy and with a personal style and vision. In the process she suggests that Gregory developed Augustine's language for communicating ideas about theology and philosophy:

> The ideas about the nature of language which Augustine developed form the basis of the theology and philosophy of the West in the Middle Ages; they gave direction to the study of the liberal arts and the exegesis they were designed to assist. It was Gregory who drew together the elements of this system and made a working synthesis of them; the principle that all God does is a communication of himself to rational beings; that God himself is language; that communication may go inwardly in a man's mind and soul, or outwardly, by showing him things his eyes can see or telling him things his ears can hear. Thus all divine communication has its inward and outward aspects.[83]

Certainly this summary of the nature of God's communication is in agreement with the conclusions of the essential features of Gregory's spirituality reached in this study. But both Gregory and Augustine echoed in their thought and lives something more; St John's idea that 'God is love'. He communicates Himself as 'love' through grace; the presence of the Holy Spirit within the soul that frees it to understand His will.

Gregory's spirituality was communicated as the product of his times. Unlike Augustine, he was deprived of the great stimulus to independent thought which

---

[81] *Ibid.*, vol.2, 294. See Butler, *Western mysticism*, 175, for example: 'the borrowing has been done with much judgement and skill, the very marrow of Augustine's thought having been extracted, shorn of its rhetoric and eloquence, and expressed in simple terms of dignity and weight — indeed a model of condensation'.

[82] *Ibid.*, vol.2, 291.

[83] G.R. Evans, *The thought of Gregory the Great* (Cambridge: Cambridge University Press, 1986), 153. This view is similar to that of Abbot Butler. See above.

polemical discussion provides. In the last decade of the sixth century there was a lull in religious controversy.[84] Nevertheless he was faced with the great pastoral challenge of a disintegrating society and a demoralised populace. Augustine had taught in his great epic, *De Civitate Dei,* that the principle role of the state was to secure civil order in which the members of the intermingled 'earthly' and 'heavenly' cities might co-exist in peace; 'peace', that is, conceived as a distorted image of the 'heavenly' peace in which the soul might at last find rest.[85] Despite the sack of Rome in 410, which occasioned the work, it was inconceivable to his contemporaries that the *Pax Romana* was about to collapse. He was concerned initially in refuting the charge that the Christian faith was responsible for Rome's misfortunes. However that theme was extended to the problem of how the Christian might co-exist with a secular power that bore the defaced image of 'fallen' humanity. He advocated the pilgrim existence; to live in the world but not of it. Gregory faced a different problem; not co-existence with the values of a powerful state but how to live as a Christian where order had collapsed and the state was unable to secure even an 'earthly' peace, which Augustine had considered was better than no peace at all to enable Christian life to flower. Gregory's contemporaries were faced with the challenge, not so much of living in the world as pilgrims where the dangers of 'worldliness' were ever present, but of living in a world where existence itself was the problem. Gregory was able to establish an ecclesiastical polity that provided Christians with the opportunity, in practising neighbourly love, to play a constructive role in re-building the morale of Roman society. In so doing he enhanced not only the prestige of the Papacy but of the Church itself, as the bulwark of society.

It was a time that called for a great preacher, teacher and spiritual leader. This is what Gregory was and why his own influence in the Middle Ages, as a transmitter and populariser of St Augustine's thought as a practical basis for an active Christian life in troubled times, was considerable. If St Augustine taught Christians they were 'in transit' in this life, Gregory taught that the time spent 'in transit' could and should be fruitful.

---

[84] Dudden, *Gregory the Great*, vol.2, 287.

[85] Augustine, *City of God* (*De civitate Dei*), London: Dent, 1950, vol. II, bk xix, 231-267. Sir Ernest Barker's 'Introduction' to this edition is an excellent guide to the themes of this work. He regards Book 19 as a good overview of the content of the whole work. See section IV. In the background of Augustine's thought on relations between Church and State lurks the problem of the Donatists in his own diocese.

See also Serge Lancel, *St Augustine* (London: SCM Press, 2002), 391-412, and Peter Brown, *Augustine of Hippo* (London: Faber & Faber, 1979), 287-329.

CHAPTER III

WILLIAM OF ST THIERRY

The Mystical Transvaluation of Augustinian Themes

William of St Thierry's role in the controversies of the twelfth century led to his dismissal by Henry Osborne Taylor as 'Bernard's jackal' and his writings were dubbed 'monkish hysteria'.[1] Since that time William's reputation has been restored. Dom Odo Brooke has referred to him as the 'Irenaeus of the twelfth century, the champion of orthodoxy and tradition'.[2] Gilson calls him 'a very great theologian' who 'has everything; power of thought, the orator's eloquence, the poet's lyricism, and all the attractiveness of the most ardent and tender piety' and who 'in the midst of his unreserved admiration for the Abbot of Clairvaux, knew how to preserve an absolute independence of thought'.[3] The purpose of this discussion is not to evaluate William's role in these controversies but to attempt to understand the interaction between the challenges he faced and his spiritual teaching and also the manner in which 'the purest representative of Augustinian thought in the twelfth century'[4] developed that inheritance.

Three aspects of the circumstances of William's life will form the skeleton on which the discussion is to be based. The first is that William was a monk; then that he was a friend and admirer of St Bernard; and finally that he was the

---

[1] H.O.Taylor, *The mediaeval mind: A history of the development of thought and emotion in the Middle Ages*, London: Macmillan, 1911, Vol. 2, 169: fn.1; 344.

[2] Odo Brooke, *Studies in monastic theology*, Kalamazoo: Cistercian Publications, 1980, 4.

[3] E. Gilson, *The mystical theology of St Bernard*, (trans. A.H.C. Downes) New York: Sheed & Ward, 1940, 198.

[4] J.M. Déchanet, 'Les maitres et les modèles: Guillaume de St Thierry', in: *La Vie Spirituelle* 53 (1937), 40-41 quoted by David N. Bell, *The image and the likeness: The Augustinian spirituality of William of St Thierry*, Kalamazoo: Cistercian Publications, 1984, 251: fn.1;. and 18: fn.19. It should be noted that Déchanet resiled from this position to some degree. One year later he says, 'but it remains obvious that an interpretation of William in the light of Augustine alone will always be lacking and will not permit us to grasp the true heart of his doctrine' (J.M. Déchanet, 'A propos de la Lettre aux Fréres du Mont-Dieu', in: *Collectanea Ordinis Cisterciensium Reformatorum* 5 (1938), 93). Déchanet, however, does not provide an unequivocal view of the 'true heart' of William's doctrine.

opponent of Abelard and William of Conches, a circumstance which brought down
on him the wrath of H.O. Taylor.[5] The thesis is that each of these circumstances
has a particular bearing on the development of William's spiritual teaching.

The relevance of the first factor, his decision to become a monk, is that in
doing so he entered a *schola caritatis* (school of love) as the monastery was
regarded.[6] There are in turn a number of factors stemming from this decision
which have significance. The first concerns his motivation for turning his back
on the great possibilities of a secular career to which his academic achievements
might have led; secondly there is the tradition he encountered at St Niçoise, a
Benedictine house; and thirdly there is the circumstance that he was elected
Abbot of St Thierry in 1119 and remained so for fifteen years.[7]

The second factor, William's admiration and friendship for St Bernard, is of
central significance for the development of his contribution to Cistercian mysticism.[8] It brought him into first hand contact with the ideals of the Cistercian
reform; it led to his involvement in the controversy between the white and black
monks; and it led him to seek to join St Bernard at Clairvaux[9] and eventually
to resign the abbacy at St Thierry and join the newly established Cistercian foundation at Signy in the Ardennes.[10]

The controversy with Abelard and William of Conches, which is the third factor, was an aspect of the continuing debate to delimit the boundaries of faith
and reason.[11] It had its destructive facet in the polemical writings to which it gave
rise. More importantly for present purposes, it also had a constructive outcome.
It led to the articulation of the theological basis of the Cistercian quest for

---

[5]   The two polemical works of William were *Disputatio adversus Petrum Abaelardum* (PL 180:
      249-282), and *De erroribus Guillelmi de Conchis* (PL180: 333-340).

[6]   For an excellent discussion of this theme, see Gilson, *The mystical theology of St Bernard*, Chap-
      ter 3. William also uses the term 'Haec [*sc.* the monastery] est specialis caritatis schola'. See
      Bell, *The image and likeness*, 208: fn.133.

[7]   J.M. Déchanet, *William of St Thierry: The man and his work*, (trans. Richard Strachan) Kala-
      mazoo: Cistercian Publications, 1972, 6-9.

[8]   Gilson, *The mystical theology of St Bernard*, Appendix V. See also Déchanet, *William of
      St Thierry*, 158, 159 and 159: fn.31 for a judgement about Gilson's brilliant note on William
      in the Appendix to his study of St Bernard.

[9]   Déchanet, *William of St Thierry*, 15: fn.51. 'For all its glorious past, the low ebb which the Order
      of Cluny had unquestionably reached, by contrast with Citeaux, when Abbot Pontius of Melgueil
      died (1122) has been brought out with admirable objectivity by Dom U. Berlière OSB'.

[10] *Ibid.*, 43: 'the author of the Vita informs us that William, drawn to the plain life of the Cister-
      cian Order and longing for solitude and spiritual quiet, laid aside the burden and dignity of an
      abbot, 'onus et honorem', and donned the holy habit of poverty at Signy'. See also p. 43, fn.2.

[11] Déchanet, *William of St Thierry*, 63: '[N]othing so much alarmed William as the blithe cock-
      sureness with which Master Peter passed unblushing censure on the oracles of Christian faith'.
      Of William of Conches, Déchanet, *ibid.*, 63: fn. 73 quotes E. Gilson, *La philosophie au Moyen
      Age*, Paris; Payot, 1930, 64: '[H]e seems to think no longer in order to understand his faith
      as St Anselm did, but for the sheer pleasure of thinking'.

perfection and its rewards; the exposition of the meaning of Cistercian trinitarian mysticism which extended and explored the boundaries of the Augustinian inheritance.[12]

These circumstances of William's life provide only a framework, a model, to assist with the analysis of the complex evolution of his thought. The challenges he faced overlap and interact. There were other less obvious but equally important influences.[13]

Above all, it is important to keep in mind the context of William's life. It spanned a period starting some time in the last quarter of the eleventh century and ended in 1148.[14] Geographically it was bounded by Liège where he was born and the Ardennes where he died; by Laon where he was, perhaps, educated or Reims, where it has been traditionally held he was educated and, more certainly, where he joined the Benedictines at St Niçoise; by St Thierry, close to Reims, where he was abbot; to the south, the bound was probably Clairvaux where he visited St Bernard. In both time and place his life was contiguous with the emerging twelfth-century renaissance.[15]

---

[12] *Ibid.*, 70-94 for a discussion of *The mirror of faith* and *The enigma of faith* as a positive response to the innovators.

[13] Gilson, *The mystical theology of St Bernard*, 13. Referring to the wave of mysticism, already perceptible round about 1125, which burst in full force on the twelfth century, he writes: 'The birth of the movement is a problem as pressing as that of vernacular literature or of ogival art; it is just as much a part of history and in no way less difficult to solve. The truth is that problems of this kind are never open to any one solution because such movements depend on very complex material conditions, with which we are very imperfectly acquainted, and especially on spiritual conditions which are so much more mysterious as their spirituality is the more pure. Let us say above all that before being effects these movements are events which suffice to themselves, until in the end they become causes. What we do know is this: that about 1120, in the Benedictine monastery of St Thierry, the Liégeois, William, began to write, or at least to consider, a '*De natura et dignitate amoris*' and that towards 1125 St Bernard addressed to some Carthusians in response to certain '*Meditationes*', all burning with divine love, an '*Epistola de Caritate*' which he was soon to incorporate in his '*De diligendo Deo*'. Beyond the field of this theology, the passionate drama of Héloise and Abelard, more fertile in ideas than one might suppose, riveted all eyes on the problem of love. There then, at any rate, we have so many events. For the rest we may still hope for some insight into the historical conditions which, if they did not determine, at least occasioned the movement. A new mystical Springtide burgeoned in the twin gardens of St Thierry and Citeaux. Whence came the fresh sap that brought it to birth?'

[14] Bell, *The image and the likeness*, 19, and fn.20 'Until recently, the opinion of André Adam and Dom Déchanet that William was born at Liège about 1085-90 and studied at Laon was rarely questioned, but the perspicacious researches of Stanislaus Ceglar have demanded that these ideas be revised. There is now growing acceptance of the hypothesis that William almost certainly studied at Reims, and that he was most probably born rather earlier than either Adam or Déchanet have suggested. Beyond this, the story of his life is well known'.

[15] See R.W. Southern, *Western society and the church in the Middle Ages*, Harmondsworth: Penguin Books, 1970, 34-44 for a masterly survey of what he calls 'The Age of Growth c. 1050-1300' in which he eschews the word 'Renaissance'.

Yet, whether or not the term 'renaissance' is used to describe the process deriving from the events of the period, it was a time in which the study of Latin classical literature received vigorous attention and may perhaps have provided the stimulus for the torrent of creativeness which, in this period, as Haskins has pointed out, produced the works which occupy a quarter of the two hundred and seventeen volumes of the *Latin Patrologia*.[16]

Moreover, the area in which William lived also overlapped the region which Panofsky identifies with the origins of what he calls the proto-Renaissance of the twelfth century.[17]

---

[16] C.H. Haskins, *The Renaissance of the twelfth century*, Cambridge MA: Harvard University Press, 1939, 6.

'More profitably we may limit the phrase to the history of culture in this age – the complete development of Romanesque Art and the rise of Gothic; the full bloom of vernacular poetry, both lyric and epic; and the new learning and new literature in Latin. The century begins with the flourishing age of the cathedral schools and closes with the earliest universities already well established at Salerno, Bologna, Paris, Montpellier and Oxford. It starts with only the bare outlines of the seven liberal arts and ends in possession of the Roman and Canon law, the new Aristotle, the new Euclid and Ptolemy, and the Greek and Arabic physicians, thus making possible a new philosophy and a new science. It sees a revival of the Latin classics, of Latin prose, and of Latin verse, both in the ancient style of Hildebert and the new rhymes of the Goliardi and the formation of liturgical drama. New activity in historical writing reflects the variety and amplitude of a richer age – biography, memoir, court annals, the vernacular history, and the city chronicle. A library circa 1100 would have little beyond the Bible and the Latin Fathers, with their Carolingian commentators, the service books of the church and various lives of the saints, the text-books of Boethius and some others, bits of local history, and perhaps certain of the Latin classics, too often covered with dust. About 1200, or a few years later, we should expect to find, not only more and better copies of these older works, but also the Corpus Juris Civilis and the classics partially rescued from neglect; the canonical collections of Gratian and the recent popes; the theology of Anselm and Lombard and other monastic leaders (a good quarter of the two hundred and seventeen volumes of the Latin Patrologia belong to this period); a mass of new history, poetry and correspondence; the philosophy, mathematics and astronomy, unknown to the earlier mediaeval tradition and recovered from the Greeks and Arabs in the course of the twelfth century. We should now have the great feudal epics of France and the best of the Provençal lyrics, as well as the earliest works in Middle High German. Romanesque art would have reached and passed its prime, and the new Gothic style would be firmly established at Paris, Chartres, and lesser centres in the Île de France'.

See also Friedrich Heer, *The mediaeval world*, New York: Praeger, 1962, 79ff:

'Twelfth century humanism, delighting in the world, in books, and in argument, revolved all the while round man himself; it was anthropocentric, seeing no sense in philosophising over God and nature unless man himself was also in the picture... Theology postulates, and must include, anthropology, the study of man'.

[17] E. Panofsky, *Renaissance and renascences in Western art*, London: Paladin, 1970, 55ff. Panofsky sees the twelfth century Renaissance as two movements; one South European and artistic; one North European and humanistic. Our point is that William's life was lived in an area in which these movements would have overlapped.

It is not possible in the present context to attempt to examine all the possible indirect effects which the changing interests of the times may have had upon William. Both St Bernard and Abelard are, of course, themselves key figures in the creative movements of the first part of the century.[18] Suffice it to recognise that William was educated and lived at a time and in places where complex cultural changes were underway. This discussion is however based on a simplifying model, which while neglecting many interesting themes will nevertheless account for the major and obvious ones.

Schola Caritatis

The circumstances which led William to decide to enter the religious life remain a matter for speculation. There is no hint of a spectacular conversion experience. It is probable that as a man of powerful intellect and a reflective, even mystical, nature, the cloister provided an appealing environment in which to pursue his studies. The boisterous atmosphere of the schools would have had little appeal and it appears he lacked ambition for worldly success. The religious life may well have been the natural choice for a devout scion of a noble family.[19] On the other hand, there may have been a point of decision which he would subsequently reflect on in terms of St Augustine's experience, for there appears to have been a considerable attraction to and empathy with St Augustine's teaching.[20]

By the time William joined the community at St Niçoise in approximately 1116, the rule of St Benedict had established a tradition extending over nearly six centuries of practice. By no means uniform, it still depended upon the interpretation of the individual abbot. St Niçoise, in the early twelfth century had a

---

[18] C.N. Brooke, *The twelfth century Renaissance*, London: Thames and Hudson, 1969, 138:
   'Bernard himself, and a few others of his kind, shared to the full the interest in human emotion and its expression which is one aspect of twelfth century humanism. In this, unintentionally and half-consciously, Bernard and Abelard were at one though the difference remained profound, since in Bernard's thought the love of man for man counted only as a shadow of the love of God for man, and its expression could only be justified by its subservience to the love of God. Yet however that may be, the sense of human love in his famous lament for his brother, or the sense of human contact which we can still feel after eight centuries in the best of his letters, makes Bernard's the most effective witness of human self-expression of his age'.

[19] Déchanet, *William of St Thierry*, 6, quoting Adam, *Guillaume de Saint-Thierry* (Bourg-en Bresse, 1923), 29-30: 'Was it out of intellectual frustration, or an instinctive distaste for the unsettled, rollicking life that has always characterised big centers of learning; or did personal relationships and influences carry the day? All are reasonable guesses, but no more than guesses'.

[20] Déchanet, *William of St Thierry*, 8. 'On the morrow of his conversion William felt his soul throb in unison with that of the man who had written the Confessions'. Empathy there was but the source of it is speculation.

good name,[21] and its fervour contrasted with the listlessness which infected many black monks. 'It was a busy center of religious life and intellectual culture'.[22] He revelled in St Augustine, St Gregory, St Ambrose and the Venerable Bede; 'especially St Augustine (…) no more luminous interpreter of Augustinian thought would emerge during the Middle Ages'.[23] In 1119 William was elected Abbot of St Thierry which bears out what is said in the *Vita Antiqua* about the reputation both he and his brother had established at St Niçoise.[24]

Monastic life had flourished at St Thierry since the sixth century[25] but Benedictine monks had not settled it permanently until 973. It was well endowed, a fact which William was to find wearisome and a constant distraction, and which emphasises the contemplative orientation of his vocation and the absence of interest in affairs. Like St Augustine and St Gregory he took upon himself the administrative duties of his office with reluctance but at the same time carried them out with zeal.[26] On the other hand, the traditional tension, as reflected in the teaching of St Augustine and St Gregory, between the calls of the contem-

---

[21] *Vita Antiqua*, (ed. A. Poncelet), in: *Mélanges Godefroid Kurth*, vol. 1, (Liège: Liège University Press, 1908), 89, 'bone opinionis tunc erat'.

[22] Adam, *Guillaume de Saint-Thierry*, 30 and Déchanet, *William of St Thierry*, 7: fn.23. Jordan had been Abbot of St Niçoise since 1108. His monastery produced leading men like Geoffrey, William's predecessor at St Thierry, who became abbot of St Médard at Soissons and then Bishop of Chalons; Drogo, Abbot of St Jean at Laon and Cardinal of Ostia; and Arnulph, who ruled the abbey of St Niçoise for some time and then withdrew to Signy shortly before William did. This latter point may have had some influence on William's own decision to join the community at Signy.

[23] Déchanet, *William of St Thierry*, 8 and fn.24. See also note 4 above. Déchanet remarks that in time his patristic reading would range farther, giving his emotional Western mind more the speculative cast of the Greek Fathers but that it always bore the indelible mark of those first contacts. He argues that this is illustrated by comparing *On Contemplating God* (begun at St Niçoise) with the *Meditations* (completed at Signy); the former so Augustinian in its preoccupation with inner states and processes, while in the latter a much more reasoned and theologically based spirituality displaces the emotive, psychological one – 'every page breathes the mysticism of Pseudo-Dionysius'. This theme of Déchanet's about Greek influences in William has been challenged by Bell (*The image and likeness*, 14ff.) and John Anderson in the introduction to his translation of the *Enigma of faith*, Kalamazoo: Cistercian Publications, 1974 (Cistercian Fathers series 9).

[24] *Vita Antiqua*, 89 and Déchanet, *William of St Thierry*, 8: fn.26. It is thought that William and his brother Simon entered St Nicoise together. Simon was elected abbot of St Nicoise aux Bois at about the same time as William's election to St Thierry. No doubt their influence upon each other would have been considerable.

[25] Déchanet, *William of St Thierry*, 9: fn.29. St Thierry, a disciple of St Remi (Remigius), is said to have settled on Mont d'Hor about 533 and King Thierry I to have endowed the monastery where many miracles took place. See J. Mabillon, *Annales* OSB, [480-1157] 6 Vols., Paris, 1703-1739, I, 64.

[26] Déchanet, *William of St Thierry*, 9: fn.31. His source is *Annales* OSB, III, 622 and V, 269-270.

plative and active lives is not prominent in that of William. He is a contemplative writing for contemplatives.

The works which date from the early part of his abbacy illustrate his idea of the monastic life and its ideal. *On the Nature and Dignity of Love* stresses the cenobitic aspect of the ideal as taken over outright, both letter and spirit, from the form of common life that Christ's first disciples led. The first object of the rule is to create that 'oneness of body and mind out of which the queen of virtues, charity, will flower'.[27] The work is thought to be based on talks given to his monks to help them achieve the ideal of perfection of charity which St Benedict sets as the one goal and reward for the practice of asceticism. The other work from this period is *On Contemplating God*. As Déchanet points out, it resembles St Augustine's *Soliloquies* and indeed part of the Praemium 2 comes word for word from St Augustine's *Confessions* x, 25, 36 and x, 36, 38.[28]

William defines love in the purest Augustinian terms. There is no hint anywhere of St Bernard's profoundly original idea. Instead of making free-will the root of love like him, William goes back to memory, 'a recollection that is a presence and, as it were, a living stamp, the very presence of the living God, the stamp of his goodness and power'.[29] Apprenticeship in 'charity' is in essence exploitation by mind and will of the privilege of being created in God's image. It is not as in St Bernard a purification and sublimation of 'sensible love' into 'spiritual' love. Indeed, William seems to rule out any compromise between human love and love which has God for its object.[30] In the preface to the *On the Nature and Dignity of Love* he says:

> The art of arts is the art of love. It is jealously taught by nature and God, the author of nature. Instilled in the very depths of the human soul by the Creator, this love which has its native country in God, keeps its exalted rank intact in the soul so long as adulterous attachments do not defile it, remaining its own master.[31]

Then he refers to the *pondus* (gravity) metaphor: 'the spirit of man tends upwards and the body tends downwards', and so, 'Since the fall, a man needs pedagogues to put him back on the road to happiness his love craves. Obviously he need not be taught a love that nature has taught him; it is simply a matter of putting right what has become tainted in him, what turns him aside from his true goal'.

For William the only genuine and natural love is love directed to God. He contrasts genuine love with fleshly love:

---

[27] Déchanet, *William of St Thierry*, 10 and fn.36.
[28] *Ibid.*, 11: fn.39.
[29] *Ibid.*, 12.
[30] *Ibid.*
[31] *De natura et dignitate amoris*, 1-2 (PL 184: 379C-382A), quoted by Déchanet, *William of St Thierry*, 12, 13. The other quotations which follow have the same source.

In the past fleshly love, impure love, had its preceptors. And what preceptors they were – shameless poets so schooled in Ovid's vile ways that their verse stands forth as a mere re-issue of his. Having inflamed men's passions they contrived 'love-cures', as that 'doctor of the art of love' had done (...) men lost to decency, wretches swamped by floods of fleshly concupiscence, in whom the order of nature perished.

The significance of this contrast is perhaps twofold. It is the reaction of a man who has recently left behind him an academic world which was rejoicing in the revival of classical literature, some aspects of which he found distasteful, to enter the contemplative world to seek true wisdom. In that world he meets St Augustine of the *Confessions* with whom he forms an immediate empathy in both his attitude to fleshly concupiscence and also the pursuit of wisdom. It is therefore perhaps natural that he should absorb St Augustine's analysis of the problem of the pursuit of true wisdom.[32]

In *On Nature and Dignity of Love*, William arranges the stages of love on an ascending scale, *voluntas* (will), *amor* (love), *caritas* (charity), *sapientia* (wisdom),[33] the summit being wisdom. There are other later references to the same idea; in the *Meditations*, 'charity is the characteristic of wisdom and the beginning of wisdom is fear of the Lord',[34] and in the commentary of the *Song of Songs*, 'the particular dwelling of love' is the *cella vinaria* (wine store) and that 'is the store of wisdom'.[35] St Augustine also believed 'wisdom is the love of God'.[36]

The nature of 'wisdom' and 'love of God' lead to a consideration of the mystical experience and the formulation of a mystical theology which are the subject of the following two sections. It is here that influences other than St Augustine become more prominent. Augustine's influence remains, perhaps, the integrating factor and his thought the foundation on which William builds.

This point is illustrated by the development of William's thought on the relationship and distinction between the terms 'voluntas', 'amor' and 'caritas'. His mature thought is contained in the *Golden Epistle*, written late in his life, from Signy to the Carthusians at Mont Dieu. There are three passages of relevance:

---

[32] Déchanet, *William of St Thierry*, 14. 'In those pages William roughs out a real treatise on the indwelling in us of the three divine Persons, making the utmost of St Augustine's doctrine of the image of God. A whole metaphysics of love emerges from it (...) they found a concentrated synthesis of St Augustine's best thinking on the love of God'.

[33] *De natura et dignitate amoris* (PL 184: 382B): 'Primum enim ad Deum voluntas animam movet, amor promovet, caritas contemplatur, sapientia fruitur'. There is a certain vagueness about the difference between *caritas* and *sapientia*; *sapientia* implies 'fruitive rest' in God while *caritas* is still in progress though at a very advanced stage.

[34] *Meditativae orationes* (PL 180): meditation, 13,6. Quoted by Bell, *Image and likeness*, 149: fn. 96, 'caritas propria sapientia, et principium sapientiae timor Domini'.

[35] *Expositio super Cantica Canticorum* (*Cant.*, PL 180: 48Th): 'Cella vinaria sapientiae est'.

[36] St Augustine, *Epistulae*, 140, 45. (PL 33: 557): 'Sapientia est caritas Dei'.

Simplicity is the naked will [turned] to God; [it is] not yet formed by reason to be love (amor) which is a formed will (formata voluntas) nor yet illumined as to be charity, which is the delight (jocunditas) of love[37]

and then:

When [the will] stretches upwards like fire going to its own place – that is, when it is joined (sociatur) with truth and is moved (movetur) to higher things it is 'amor'. When it is suckled by grace so that it might be moved on (promovetur), it is 'dilectio', when it seizes [its object], when it takes hold [of it], when it enjoys [it], it is 'caritas', it is 'unitas spiritus' (spiritual union), it is God, for God is charity.[38]

In the following sentence William indicates 'final perfection of this is not possible in this present life'. The notion of *dilectio* has now been inserted between those of *amor* and *caritas*, suggesting another distinguishable staging post along the way.

The third passage goes further:

'Amor' is a strong will to God (magna voluntas ad Deum); 'dilectio', a clinging (adhaesio) [to him] or conjunction (conjunctio) [with him]; 'caritas', fruition. But for the man who has his heart on high, unity of spirit with God is the perfection of the will that progresses into God, when not only does it will what God wills, but is so much not affected but perfected in affection, that it cannot will anything save that which God wills.[39]

For William there is clearly all the mystery and pleasure of surprise in the progress of this loving relationship with God which is the goal of the *schola caritatis*. But in attempting to distinguish staging posts in the growth of love he is well aware that the terms or signposts used are not in themselves important: the point is illustrated in his commentary on the *Song of Songs*:

For [*the Song of Songs*] is concerned with 'amor' of God, or [the love] by which God is loved, or by which God himself is called 'amor', which, whether it be called 'amor' or 'caritas' or 'dilectio' is not of importance, except that in the name 'amor' there seems to be indicated a certain tender 'affectus' (affection) [on the part] of one who loves or strives or entreats; in the name 'caritas' a certain spiritual 'affectio', or the joy of fruition; in 'dilectio' a natural desire (appetitus) for a

---

[37] Bell, *Image and likeness*, 149: fn.97. Source, *Epistola ad fratres de Monte Dei*, 3l7A (*Ep. Frat.*, Sources Chretiennes (SC) 49), 'Vel simplicitas, sola est ad Deum voluntas, scilicet nondum ratione formata, ut amor sit, id est formata voluntas, nondum illuminata, ut sit caritas, hoc est amoris jocunditas'.

[38] *Ibid.*, 150: fn.98. *Ep. Frat.*, 345A (SC 235): 'Haec, cum sursum tendit, sicut ignis amor est; cum, ut promoveatur, lactatur a gratia, dilectio est; cum apprehendit, cum tenet, cum fruitur, caritas est, unitas spiritus est. Deus est, Deus enim caritas est'.

[39] *Ibid.*, 151: fn.99. *Ep. Frat.*, 348A-B (SC 257).

delectable object. Nevertheless, one and the same Spirit works all these things, in
the love of the Bridegroom and the Bride.[40]

In this passage William is exploring the language of the love of God. In the last
resort however the terms themselves are not important because they are phases
within an ascending continuum, through which the Holy Spirit progressively
manifests itself. The sense of mystery and of joy, as the mystery is discovered, or
rather, revealed, are conveyed in the traditional symbolism of the Bride and
Bridegroom.

This notion of a continuum is consistent with William's view in the *On the
Nature and Dignity of Love* that the ascent of love is not *per gradus* (by steps):

> Every wise person that ascends should understand that these grades of ascension
> (voluntas, amor, caritas, sapientia) are not like the rungs of a ladder, in as much
> as particular affections are necessary at certain times but not at others. In the
> order of ascent, each single 'affectus' (affection) has its time and place by which,
> in cooperation with other affections, it seems to accomplish its own part more dili-
> gently. But all of them run together (concurrere) and cooperate, preceding and
> following [one another], and often the first becomes the last and the last first.[41]

In the *Meditations* he suggests the reason:

> Therefore, O Lord, your love (amor) is always in the soul of your poor one, but
> [it is] latent (latens) like fire under ashes, until the Spirit, who blows where he
> wills [John 3:8], should be pleased to manifest it profitably as and to the extent
> he wills.[42]

In the passages from William's works which have been discussed he analyses the
progress of the relationship with God from its beginnings as an 'image', latent
as it were, towards a 'likeness', where God is fully revealed in the soul. In this
analysis he seems to be articulating his own experiences in Augustinian terms,
by relating them to Augustine's. There is also an Augustinian preoccupation
with, as Bell put it, 'precisely how we can explain our cooperation with God'. It
remains logically inexplicable. God it is who operates, but as William says, man
is *in opere* (in the working),[43] a phrase which seems to indicate clearly that God
works in and through man. There is no explanation of just how this is so. But
the soul does cooperate until it is rapt by the Holy Spirit into such an inexpress-

---

[40] *Ibid.*, 152: fn.l00. *Expositio super Cantica canticorum* (*Cant.*), 475B-C (SC 6).

[41] *Ibid.*, 157, 158: fn.109. *De natura et dignitate amoris* (PL 184: 408A-B).

[42] *Ibid.*, 158: fn.112. *Meditativae orationes* (PL 180: 248C, med.,12,18).

[43] *Ibid.*, 147 and 165: fn.l34. *Cant.*, 508B (SC 100), '[E]t iam amando Deum homo quidem est
in opere, sed Deus est qui operatur. Non enim Paulus, sed gratia Dei secum'. We may compare Augustine *De natura et gratias*, 31.35 (PL 44: 264), 'Ubi quidem operamur et nos: sed
illo operante cooperamur'.

ible communion with God that it may be spoken of as being of 'One Spirit'.[44] It is in his analysis of the state of *unitas spiritus* that William seems to go beyond Augustine. For Augustine is fascinated by the problem of the 'Image of God' in man, whereas St Bernard's fascination is with the achievement of the 'Likeness'. It is perhaps in William's intense interest in the same problem as St Bernard that the influence of their relationship may be felt. For William, like St Bernard, was concerned in the *schola caritatis* to seek the ideal of perfection which should be the end of the contemplative life.

'The Likeness'

The admiration which William felt for St Bernard is evident from his *Vita Bernardi*. It was an admiration and fascination which dated from their first meeting when William was still a novice at St Niçoise. Bernard also had the highest regard for William; he became Bernard's confidant, his second self.[45] The following passage illustrates the relationship and much else besides:

> I was unwell at St Thierry, drained of strength and quite worn out by an illness that dragged on and on. When the man of God heard the news he sent his brother, Gerard, of blessed memory, to bid me come to Clairvaux. He assured me that once there I would speedily either regain my health or die. As for myself, seizing the opportunity God seemed to offer me of dying in his company (which then appealed to me more I really cannot say), I set out immediately and reached Clairvaux weary and in pain. The promise that had been made to me came true – the one I hoped for at heart. My health was restored; by degrees my strength came back. Merciful God, what benefits that illness brought me – that rest, that freedom from every care. They satisfied my longing. Bernard's illness itself worked for my own good, while I lay ill beside him. Flat on our backs, the two of us, we spent the (…) day talking about the spiritual nature of the soul (de spirituali physica animae) and the cures which virtue furnishes for the illnesses of vice. It was then, so far as the length of my illness allowed, that he expounded the *Song of Songs* to me; though only in the moral sense, without launching upon the mysteries with which the book abounds. This was what I hoped for, what I had asked him to do. Every day for fear of forgetting the things I had heard, I put them down insofar as God enabled me to and my memory served me. Thus I shared the insights of the man of God. As good-natured and disinterested as you please, he disclosed his ideas to me as they came to mind and the meanings that his experience enabled him to make out. He outdid himself enlightening my utter ignorance of things that can only be known from personal experience. I could not as yet grasp all that

---

[44] *Ibid.*, 165.
[45] Déchanet, *William of St Thierry*, 24: fn.74, and 25: fn.77. 'Suus ille quod suus'.

he told me; but listening to him I realised as never before how far above me those lofty truths still soared.[46]

The whole passage illuminates the closeness of the relationship between the two men. In particular, the last two sentences are significant. 'The things that can be known only from personal experience' are doubtless the description of the mystical experience associated with the state of *unitas spiritus*. St Augustine had described such experiences but the first-hand account from St Bernard must have made a deep impression. Perhaps it inspired the future direction of William's spiritual development;[47] his thwarted desire to join Bernard at Clairvaux and ultimately its partial realisation in joining the Cistercian community of Signy;[48] his cooperation with St Bernard in the attempt to revitalise the black monks, of which Bernard's *Apology to William of St Thierry* bears witness;[49] and ultimately to developing a mystical theology to explain the nature of the mystical experience.

To understand the role of Cistercian spirituality, which St Bernard exemplified, in William's teaching, it is useful to compare it with that of the black monks, the order of which William was a member. Rupert of Deutz well represents the position of the black monks.[50] He viewed the mysteries of Christianity more in the broad outlines of the history of salvation in contrast to the Cistercians who dwelt principally on the reflection of this history as experienced within the individual soul. To this extent the Cistercians also reflect what Panofsky has called the proto-humanist renaissance of the twelfth century, however much they may react against the ideas of sensible love which characterised it. In emphasising the theme of the journey of the individual soul to God, they accented also the importance of the individual in the scheme of salvation.

Louis Bouyer has summed it up in *La Spiritualité' de Citeaux* as 'une dynamique de l'âme' (a dynamic of the soul), a movement directed to a state of 'likeness', the experience of the Trinity which foreshadows the final vision of

---

[46] Déchanet, *William of St Thierry*, 25-27 quotes *Vita Bernardi*, I, 12, 59-60.

[47] Déchanet, *William of St Thierry*, 28: fn.80: Père Malevez writes, 'La doctrine d'l'Image et la connaissance mystique chez Guillaume de St Thierry', in: *Recherches de Science Religieuse* 22, (1932), 181: fn.6, 'St Bernard may have shown William his mystical vocation; certainly William owed Bernard much of the great-souled hardihood he showed in following it'.

[48] *Ibid.*, 32. St Bernard, *Epistolae* LXXXVI, 2 (PL 182: 210 CD), 'My advice is that you keep your abbacy. Stay where you are and try to be helpful to those of whom you are in charge (…) Sorry your case will be if you wield power without proving of any use; but sorrier still if you refuse to serve your fellows for fear of bearing rule'.

[49] *Ibid.*, 15-23.

[50] Brooke, *Studies in monastic theology*, 3: fn.6, quotes Rupert of Deutz's *De Trinitate* (PL 167: 199). 'In the Prologue he aims to show how the Trinity acts through the 'Book' of Creation and Redemption and divides history into three main phases attributed respectively to the Father, the Son and the Holy Spirit'. For Rupert of Deutz (c.1075-1129) see *The Oxford dictionary of the Christian church*, Oxford: Oxford University Press, 1984.

God in eternity.[51] In the *Enigma of Faith* William identifies three theological stages in the ascent to God – the way of faith, of reasoning faith (*ratio fidei*) and finally 'experience'.[52] The three stages closely parallel the three states which form the basis of his analysis of the spiritual ascent in the *Golden Epistle*; the states which he calls 'animal', 'rational' and 'spiritual'.[53] The objective, however, is to achieve 'likeness'. William's main interest and insights are in the understanding of the nature of the 'likeness' and how knowledge of it is obtained. The soul cannot know God as he knows himself unless it has been transformed into his likeness:

> To be like God (namely in the final vision) will be to see God, to know him. We shall see him, know him in the same proportion as we are like him, to the precise extent that we see him, know him. For to see God, to know him, is to be like him; and to be like him, is to see him, to know him.[54]

The riddle is explained by the notion that the soul is raised to a created participation in the life of the Holy Spirit:

> We may say that the life of the Spirit is this union, not only because the Holy Spirit effects it or that he brings man's spirit to it, but because he, the Holy Spirit, God, Love, is this union (ipsa ipse est Spiritus Sanctus). For he is the union, the sweetness and the goodness of the Father and Son; he is their kiss, their embrace and whatever is common to them both in that transcendent union which is truth, in that truth which is union. Through him, then, all that belongs to the son by substantial union in his relationship to the Father, or to the Father in his relationship to the Son – all this is given in due proportion to man in his relationship to God; and man, in the possession of this blessed experience, when Father and Son kiss and embrace, finds himself some way in their midst. Through the Holy Spirit, the man of God becomes in some ineffable, incredible way – not God exactly; but what God is by nature, man becomes by grace.[55]

Such is *similitudo*, the likeness, for William. *Caritas* which is an informed and 'pure' love, may, as and when God pleases, be transformed into *unitas spiritus* by participation, by participative grace, in some inexplicable way, to dwell within the Divine Being, to share in the love of the Father for the Son and *vice versa*.

---

[51] *Ibid.*, 4, quoting Louis Bouyer, *La spiritualité de Citeaux*, Paris: Portulan, 1954, 121.

[52] *Ibid.*, 3.

[53] *The golden epistle*, (trans. Theodore Berkeley) Kalamazoo: Cistercian Publications, 1980, 25,I,41. '[T]here are beginners, those who are making progress and the perfect. The state of beginners may be called "animal", the state of those making progress "rational" and the state of the perfect "spiritual"'.

[54] Brooke, *Studies in monastic theology*, quoting William *Speculum fidei* (PL 180: 393C).

[55] *The golden epistle*, II,X,VI, in Dom Odo Brookes' translation, quotes PL 184: 349A-B. For an alternative, see pp. 95 and 96 in Berkeley's translation.

This leads to a consideration in the following section of the notion *amor intellectus est*.

'Amor Intellectus Est'

The theological basis for the key notions of *Amor ipse intellectus est* (Love itself is understanding) and *Cognitio amoris* (knowledge-in-love) was developed by William principally in the *Mirror of Faith* and the *Enigma of Faith*.[56] The treatises were written, in part, as a positive and traditional alternative to the rationalist approach to faith of Abelard and his supporters;[57] in part to allay the confusion felt in many religious communities as a result of the exposure of the Christian mysteries to logical analysis.[58] Like much of William's opus, they were occasional pieces which provided an opportunity to work out the theology associated with the insights he received from the experiences of his own, and no doubt St Bernard's, devotional life.[59]

The proper spheres of faith and reason had been, and continued to be, a contentious topic. In the *Mirror of Faith* William clearly explains where he stands. There are things unseen that the human mind can infer from things seen. Moreover, every man has within him a stock of inborn truths which his intellect can

---

[56] *The golden epistle*. Introduction by Déchanet, xxvii: fn.48. 'According to P. Rousselot, this formula originally came from St Gregory the Great: "Dum enim audita super coelestia amamus, amata iam novimus, quia amor ipse notitia est" – Homily Twenty-seven on the Gospel, PL 76: 1207. But the idea is earlier than St Gregory. It comes from the East'.

[57] *The enigma of faith*, (trans. John S. Anderson), 9. 'The exact relationship between the two treatises and Peter Abelard is not made clear by William'.

[58] William's letter to Bernard and Geoffrey of Léves, Bishop of Chartres. *Inter opera Sti Bernardi, Epist.* CCCXXVI (PL 182: 521-533): 'He deals with divine Scripture as he used to deal with dialectic (…) He sits in judgement on faith instead of humbly learning from it'. Nowadays Abelard and his doctrine fare better but it would take us too far afield to pursue this here. Suffice it to quote D.E. Luscombe, *The school of Peter Abelard: The influence of Abelard's thought in the early Scholastic period*, Cambridge: Cambridge University Press, 1969, 308:
'He is "one who whose infallible instinct leads straight to dangerous questions and provoking replies" (E. Gilson: *Heloise and Abelard*, 105). The challenge contained in such enquiries when cultivated by an intelligence of Abelard's power is an unusually demanding one in any academic society'.

[59] In the preface to the *Golden Epistle* William says in relation to the *Mirror of Faith* and the *Enigma of Faith*:
'I took upon myself to dedicate another little work to you as well, which I had to write to console a few of my brethren and rally their faith because of misgivings (vexatious rather than dangerous) which they felt… The work I speak of comprise two short books. As it is lucid and easy I have decided to call the first the *Mirror of Faith*; the second, which concisely sets forth the groundwork and formularies of faith in the words and according to the mind of the Catholic Doctors, is a trifle difficult, and so I call it the *Enigma of Faith*'.

readily unearth and study at leisure – such as the existence of an almighty God who has made and benevolently governs all things. Strictly speaking these truths are not a matter of faith; the mind discovers them within itself by its own efforts, without any special help from grace. But quite the other way, the truths called 'revealed' – mysteries like God's oneness in a Trinity of Persons, the Incarnation of the Word, the redemption, the nature of grace – only faith can know; only the Holy Spirit can enable their meaning to be understood.[60]

The role of the Holy Spirit is the key to the understanding of how knowledge is derived from faith. As already noted the ascent to God is seen in three theological stages; the ways of faith, reasoning faith and experience. The Holy Spirit is himself the love by which God is loved – *'ipse enim est amor noster'* (for He Himself is our love). Love and knowledge are closely linked in this experience, described as knowledge-in-love (*cognitio amoris*) – meaning not a formal identification of the faculties of intellect and will, but their interpenetration and union in this knowledge of God which is sui generis, the root of which is the trinitanian life.[61]

In other words, through the Holy Spirit we share that mutual knowledge by which Father and Son know each other:

> Those to whom the Father and Son reveal each other know exactly as Father and Son know each other; that is, they have written in them the mutual knowledge that the Father and Son have of each other; they have their unity, their will and their love; and all this is the Holy Spirit.[62]

It is an experiential knowledge which foreshadows the final vision:

> The sweet awareness (sensus) and experience of this infinite good, this indeed is life, the truly blessed life – even though in this wretched life it cannot be complete.

---

[60] Déchanet, *William of St Thierry*, 74.
[61] Brooke, *Studies in monastic theology*, 3ff. Gilson comments:
'It is not surprising then that the soul 'feels' God, when it loves God; it feels Him by the very love it has for Him and by the joy it finds in it; therefore it knows God...It means therefore in the first place that in this life no sight of God is accessible to man, not even in ecstasy. The soul seizes God, but: "amatum plus quam cogitatum, gustatum quam intellectum". (*In Cant.* Cap.I: PL 184: 505-506-507C) (...) In other words, if love makes us know God inasmuch as it makes us like God, the knowledge of God that it brings amounts to the divine likeness it confers and to the joy we feel in it (...) No matter what image he uses, never then does he mean to say that charity gives us that knowledge, sight, or vision of God which here below is refused to every intelligence (...) All that William would say is that in default of a knowledge, which is and remains impossible, love, in us replaces it; which is not to say that they are one (...) Charity produces, by love, in the will, this assimilation of the soul to God which remains in this life impossible for the reason. The union of wills is therefore, in the order of love, the equivalent of the union of mind and object in the similitude of the image' (*Mystical theology of St Bernard*, 209, 210).
[62] *De contemplando Deo*, PL 184: 376B. Quoted by Brooke, *Studies in monastic theology*, 4.

But in the future life, life and happiness will be brimming over all the time, for ever.[63]

The question arises whether William is referring to a direct intuition or a theological explanation based on the memory of the experience. The latter seems more likely. Despite allusions in the writings of the Fathers to experiential knowledge of the Trinity, there was no fully developed theology of this experience. Neither Augustine nor Gregory had offered one. William evolved a theology of the Trinity which is essentially mystical and a mysticism which is essentially trinitarian.

The question which may legitimately be asked is how far does the ultimate value of the explanation depend on the initial premise; that is the theology of the Holy Spirit as the mutual love and union of the Father and the Son, a theological opinion deriving principally from St Augustine. But despite its basis in the Augustinian theory of the Holy Spirit, it throws light on the whole scriptural and 'Greek' trinitarian tradition.

William teaches that the true self is to be discovered in the life of the trinity. Created with the imprint of the trinitarian image, the soul is impelled towards the recovery of the perfect likeness of its archetype. In so far as the soul achieves that likeness it is given an insight which passes beyond all that can be known by the senses or by human reason.[64]

This is the kind of understanding which unaided reason cannot attain. It is achieved by tasting, by achieving the ultimate goal of love, *unitas spiritus*, and it is an understanding which is the gift of God. The experience of it transforms the will so that it becomes the will of God and this is the achievement of wisdom.

Reflection

William of St Thierry emerges from this study as a man of great religious warmth and insight and as an intellectual, in the best sense of the word, a rigorous and penetrating thinker; he is both a mystic and a scholastic. He has absorbed the learning of his time, its interest in the classical literary revival and in the application of Logic; yet he has not been overwhelmed by it. He savours the making of fine distinctions in his analysis of love but he also appreciates that in the last resort they are unimportant. Ultimately the mystery of faith is paramount and

---

[63] *De contemplando Deo*, PL 184: 394BC. In Brooke, *Ibid.*

[64] Brooke provides a most useful overview of William's trinitarian mysticism in Chapter 1 of his *Studies in monastic theology*.

intellect is its servant. He is the sort of man who would find an immediate empathy with St Augustine, as indeed he did with St Bernard.

It has been suggested that the circumstances of his life and times have a crucial bearing upon his spiritual orientation. At St Niçoise he encountered the great Benedictine tradition of spirituality and learning in an establishment that had retained the spirit of the tradition. The circumstances of his vocation are unclear but it is likely that his spiritual orientation was plastic, able to be moulded. He was faced with the challenge of living the ideal of perfection; his guides were St Ambrose, St Gregory and St Augustine. St Augustine, in particular, in the *Confessions* and in *De Trinitate* has the warmth and the intellectual penetration, likely to appeal to a man of William's sensitivity and intellect. His early works on 'love' and 'contemplation' reflect the extent to which he had absorbed Augustine's teaching.

The second circumstance of crucial importance was the relationship with St Bernard, whose warmth and personal charisma, had an enormous attraction for William. He embodied the ideal of perfection which William sought; and in age and intellect was William's peer. The ideal of Cistercian reform appealed to William to the extent that he seriously considered resigning his abbacy to become a monk at Clairvaux. The ideal of perfection remained the challenge but the relationship with Bernard focussed his attention on its nature. It has been suggested that it was perhaps the nature of Bernard's mystical experiences and the mystery of the 'Likeness' of God that canalised his own search for perfection.[65] The trinitarian mystical doctrine of Augustine with its development of the 'image and likeness' theme was already available as a starting point. He developed Augustine's speculation on the role of the 'Spirit' into his own doctrine of *unitas spiritus*, as a description of the manner in which the 'Likeness' is to be achieved. Whereas the orientation of St Augustine's trinitarian mysticism is christo-centric, focussed on the mystery of the Word made flesh, and on man as created in the image of God, William's was centred on the role of the Holy

---

[65] The point is that Bernard's influence, in Malevez's words, (see n.47 above) may have shown William his mystical vocation. This is not in any way intended to limit Bernard's influence on the development of spirituality in general. Butler (*Western mysticism*, London 1967, 96) remarks: 'It is Pourrat's judgement that in the sphere of personal devotional life it was St Bernard who principally shaped the Catholic piety of the later Middle Ages and also of modern times. This is especially true of his expression of tender devotional love for the Humanity of our Lord, and for his Mother'. With this view Dean Inge is in substantial accord: 'His[Bernard's] great achievement was to recall devout and loving contemplation to the image of the crucified Christ and to found that worship of Our Saviour as "bridegroom of the Soul" which in the next centuries inspired so much fervid devotion and lyrical sacred poetry'. See W.R. Inge, *Christian mysticism* (London: Methuen, 1899), 140. The contrast with this assessment of Bernard's interest with William's particular interest in the Holy Spirit emphasises the independence of William's achievement.

Spirit within the trinitarian relationship and on the great mystery of God as 'Spirit' and 'Love'. William's orientation is reflected in his great work, the *Golden Epistle*, which until the seventeenth century, was attributed to St Bernard and only in the last century has been confirmed to be William's.

The third circumstance, which, it has been suggested, extended William's Augustinian orientation, was the challenge of his rationalist contemporaries; the development of a doctrine of 'amor intellectus est' in, principally, the *Mirror* and *Enigma*, was a response to this challenge. Abelard may or may not have been a friend and fellow student of William at Laon;[66] but it is not difficult to imagine that Abelard's approach to the mysteries of faith was totally antithetical to William. It challenged his sense of reverence and humility and his deepest convictions about the respective roles of faith and reason in understanding and interpreting the Christian mysteries. In response to the challenge of Abelard, rather in the same way as Augustine had responded to Pelagius, William articulated his mystical doctrine of *amor intellectus est*. It is the notion that only in love can the mysteries of God be understood. They are felt rather than apprehended by the intellect.

William built upon the Augustinian tradition and enlarged it, moulding it to the Cistercian apprehension of the ideal of Christian perfection and wisdom. What emerged was what has been increasingly appreciated as a unique contribution to mystical theology, however much a blend of Augustinian trinitarian ideas and Cistercian idealism. In Gilson's words, 'Nowhere has the mystical transvaluation of the most familiar Augustinian themes been more happily carried out'.[67]

These great spiritual themes reflecting a tension between 'image and likeness', 'faith and reason', 'love and knowledge' are all prominent in William's teaching. Strangely those of 'joy and sorrow' and 'the contemplative and active lives' are not so prominent. The highly mystical orientation of William's spirituality with its emphasis on the Holy Spirit and 'love' suggest that 'joy' rather than 'sorrow' was his interest, a preoccupation which might be considered consistent with the optimistic mood of the time. It is in contrast with the christo-centric flavour of Augustine's teaching with an emphasis on the 'sorrow' which thought of the redemption generates, and on the 'Fall' and of man's unworthiness. However, just as Augustine also uniquely expresses the lyrical aspects of redemption, so too William is no stranger to the rigours of asceticism and self-denial on the road to achieving the ideal of perfection. The curbing of the flesh and purifying the

---

[66] Whether or not they were fellow students depends on estimates of William's date of birth and whether he studied at Laon or Reims. Despite the work of Ceglar and Anderson there is still an element of doubt.

[67] Gilson, *The mystical theology of St Bernard*, 249: fn.274.

soul are also for him the prerequisites of experiencing the joys of the mystical experience.

Similarly, William in his devotional life experienced the tension between the pull of the contemplative and active vocations; the one in carrying the burden of his office of Abbot, the other in the attraction of the eremetic life of contemplation. His teaching was concerned with living the ideal of perfection in a contemplative environment. He reflected, perhaps unconsciously, St Gregory's view that teaching others what has been revealed by God, is of the essence of the 'active' Christian life.

The other key theme in Augustine's teaching was that of 'grace and freedom'; the respective roles of God and the individual soul in the journey of the soul to God. The theme is certainly not neglected by William. Without the *capax Dei* (ability to grasp God) implanted in man by 'created' grace, the effects of the Fall would be overwhelming; without 'illuminating grace' progress in regeneration would be impossible. Yet man's freedom to realise or reject his spiritual inheritance, is the ultimate gift of grace. The choice between the attractions of the carnal and spiritual worlds creates an ever present tension in the Christian life. William does not go beyond St Augustine in his treatment of the theme but the Augustinian teaching underlies his own on the progress of the spiritual life through the states 'animal', 'rational' and 'spiritual'. In the last resort, the problem presented by the theme, is submerged by the identification of the love of God and knowledge of God and the conclusion that the love of God can only be experienced or felt, for that love is God Himself, the Holy Spirit. William recognises that the teacher can only recommend and point out the joy to be found in the spiritual life, ultimately the dynamics of the relationship between God and the individual soul is a mystery.[68]

In Augustine's words: 'Love me and you will have me but you will be unable to love me unless you possess me already',[69] is what God says to the soul.

---

[68] Bell, *The image and likeness*, 131ff. discusses William's treatment of 'grace' and the convergence of the theme of 'grace and freedom' and 'love and knowledge' in his teaching.

[69] St Augustine, *Sermon* 34, 5 (PL 38: 211): 'Amate me, et habebitis me; quia nec potestis amare me, nisi habueritis me'.

CHAPTER IV

WALTER HILTON

The Christo-centric Transvaluation of Augustinian Themes

The focus of this chapter about Walter Hilton is on the nature of his spiritual teaching as an expression of Augustinian tradition and the manner in which aspects of the tradition are transvalued in response to contemporary challenges. Hilton lived in the late fourteenth century, a particularly challenging time for the spiritual teacher, and for the last decade of his life he was an Augustinian Canon.[1] The significance of these factors requires some further explanation.

The fourteenth century was a time of spiritual unrest both in England, where Hilton lived, and in the wider Church.[2] The institutional Church, particularly the Papacy, was on the defensive; the secular powers were in the process of claiming and establishing an ascendancy.[3] The social fabric of society throughout Western Europe had been radically affected by the onset of the plague.[4] In England, the Peasants Revolt of 1381 reflected the pressures which old relationships faced as a result of new circumstances, both economic and social.[5] On the other hand, the reforms of the thirteenth century, as Pantin's work on the English Church reveals, seemed to have been highly successful in creating a section of laity much better educated in religious matters and conscientiously attempting

---

[1] He died on the Vigil of the Feast of the Annunciation, 24th March, 1396. See P. Hodgson, *Cloud of Unknowing and related treatises*, Exeter: Catholic Record Press, 1982, Introduction, x: fn.2; and also Joy Russell-Smith, 'In defense of the veneration of images', in: *Dominican Studies* 7 (1954), 180-214.

[2] Richard Kieckhefer, *Unquiet souls: Fourteenth century saints and their religious milieu*, Chicago: University of Chicago, 1984, 10. 'The hagiographers of the fourteenth century often recapture an Augustinian fascination with the inner life and an equally Augustinian sense of disquietude.

[3] 'Babylonian Captivity' of the Papacy at Avignon (1305-77) and the 'Great Schism' which began in 1378 are indicative of the problems for the Papacy, while in England, the Statutes of Provisors (1351, 1365 and 1390) and Praemunire (1353 and 1393) are illustrative of the on-going struggle between Church and State.

[4] There were two main outbreaks in England in 1348 and 1361.

[5] V.H.H. Green, *The later Plantagenets*, London: Edward and Arnold, 1955, 213-221.

to live in accordance with their more sensitive religious consciousness.[6] Intellectual currents were taking Scholasticism into its more arid reaches and Nominalism encouraged a more sceptical approach to established teaching than the dialectics of the twelfth century had done.[7] Middle English was developing rapidly as a sensitive and powerful medium for both spiritual and poetic expression and perhaps symbolised the more independent outlook of a more self-conscious sense of English identity and individuality.[8] The activities of the Lollards and the more doctrinally orientated attacks of Wyclif were as much a reflection of a new religious, intellectual and social awareness as the works of the English mystics.[9] In Hilton's case, the range of his correspondents – the anchoress of his *Scale of Perfection*, the Lord to whom the *Mixed Life* was addressed, a canon lawyer considering the religious life and Adam Horsley seeking advice about leaving the secular service of Government for the life of contemplation as a Carthusian[10] – illustrates the challenge he faced as a spiritual director to both religious and laity. The task was to adapt traditional teaching to meet new circumstances and yet reinforce orthodox Church positions in the face of the suspicions aroused by Lollard views which seemed to gain in currency as the century progressed.

As an Augustinian Canon, Hilton would have been well placed to understand the problems of adaptation faced by both the institutional Church and the laity. Moreover, the balance between institutional and pastoral life which an Augustinian community practised would probably have strengthened his awareness both of the monastic spiritual heritage and of the evangelical approach of the friars.[11]

---

[6]   E.A. Pantin, *The English Church in the fourteenth century*, Cambridge: Cambridge University Press, 1955, 250.
'The mystics in fact presuppose an audience thoroughly and severely drilled in the rudiments of faith and morals, and the widespread appeal of vernacular mystical literature in the later middle ages seems to argue that the programme of religious instruction planned by the reforming bishops of the thirteenth century did succeed in reaching and indoctrinating certain sections of the laity. If the devout and literate layman was something of a problem to the Church, he was also in some respects a product of the Church's own work'.

[7]   Frederick Copleston, *Late mediaeval and renaissance philosophy*. Part 1: *Ockham to the speculative mystics* (*A history of philosophy*. Vol.3), New York: Image Books, 1963. See the whole of the introduction and especially 21 ff.

[8]   R.W. Chambers, *On the continuity of English prose*, London 1932.

[9]   K.B. McFarlane, *John Wycliffe and the beginnings of English non-conformity*, London: English Universities Press, 1952, particularly the Prologue, 9-11 in which the problems of sources for this period are reviewed. This is an excellent account of the Lollard movement and Wycliffe's role in it.

[10] P. Hodgson, *Cloud of Unknowing*, x: fn.2. In the 'de Utilitate' letter Hilton encouraged Adam Horsley to persevere in his intention to leave the Exchequer and enter religion as a Carthusian of Beauvale Priory near Nottingham, which Horsley did c.1383-85.

[11] *Ibid.* Soon after 1383-85 Hilton became an Augustinian canon at the Priory of St Peter, Thurgarton, near Southwell, Notts. For the place of the Augustinians in Church history in the late

Such considerations in the case of Hilton are nevertheless speculative, for very little is known with certainty either about the community at Thurgarton in the fourteenth century[12] or about his life.[13]

We can only speculate about his reasons for electing to join the Augustinians. It is now thought he may have lived in the vicinity and been familiar with the community. More probably he was attracted to the Augustinian lifestyle. The Rule which carries Augustine's name was inspired by the example of the community that he established at Hippo.[14] It, in turn, had been modelled on the first apostolic community at Jerusalem (Acts 4, 31-5). The symbol of 'Jerusalem' is significant in Hilton's major work, the *Scale of Perfection*. In particular, his use of the parable of the journey to Jerusalem, with its Christic resonances, to illustrate the Christian's mystic quest, suggests he was conscious of the link between the remote origin/inspiration of his Order and the purpose of his life in the Augustinians. For example he writes: 'Jerusalem is (…) "sight of peace" and stands for contemplation in perfect love of God, for contemplation is nothing

---

Middle Ages, see J.C. Dickinson, *The origin of the Austin Canons and their introduction into England*, London 1950; and R.W. Southern, *Western society and the Church in the Middle Ages*, Harmondsworth: Penguin Books, 1983 (Pelican History of the Church 2), 241-250 and especially, 243, 244: notes 36, 37. He refers to U. Chevalier's, *Codex diplomaticus ordinis. S. Rufi Valentiae* (1891), 3 and 8-9 in relation to Pope Urban II's comments in the preamble to the Charter. Southern comments: 'In the monastic life men abandoned earthly things, and gave themselves up to contemplation. In the canonical life, they made use of earthly things, and redeemed with tears and almsgiving the daily sins inseparable from the world. The monks therefore played the part of Mary, the canons that of Martha in the Church, The role of the canons was the humbler of the two but no less necessary (…) In Urban's view, therefore, the canons had revived a neglected primitive tradition of the Church – a tradition in which practical service had a dominant place – and had restored a balance which the overwhelming success of Benedictine monasticism in the preceding centuries had destroyed'.

[12] D. Knowles & R.N. Hadcock, *Mediaeval religious houses, England and Wales*, London: Longmans, 1953, 54-55 and 156. It is estimated that the Black Death halved the numbers in every religious order. This was a large priory possibly some thirty canons in its earlier days, the gross income in 1291 being about £247. There appear to have been at least seventeen canons in 1538, the same number receiving pensions at the dissolution. S.S.Hussey, 'Walter Hilton – Traditionalist' in: Marion Glasscoe (Ed.), *Mediaeval mystical tradition in England*, Exeter: University of Exeter, 1980, 6 [hereafter referred to as M. M. T. E. with year of publication]. There is evidence from a fifteenth century manuscript referring to Hilton as canon and governor of the Priory. However, since William of Saperton was prior from 1381-1416, it is unlikely Hilton was prior. See article by Joy Russell-Smith and M.D. Knowles in the *Dictionaire de spiritualité* (Vol.7, Paris 1969) on Walter Hilton.

[13] The Introduction to the *Scale of Perfection* in the edition of J.P.H. Clark & R. Dorward (New York: Paulist Press, 1991), provides an excellent account of what is known, or can be reasonably surmised, about Hilton's life. I have relied on this work extensively in this chapter.

[14] *The Rule of Saint Augustine*, (trans. Raymond C. Canning) London: Darton, Longman & Todd, 1984. See the Introduction by Tarsicus J. Van Bavel, 7.

other than a sight of Jesus, who is true peace'.[15] Be that as it may, it is clear his works were positively influenced by his knowledge of Augustine's teaching.

Much of Augustine's teaching seems to revolve around two poles; 'reformation' and 'love' and their interdependence. On the one hand he is aware of the defaced 'image' of the divine in humanity and the need for reformation; on the other of the infinite mercy of God and of the divine 'likeness' to which individuals may aspire through 'grace'. Augustine's spirituality is suffused with a consciousness of the ubiquity of divine love which induces all movement towards a 'likeness'.

At the outset it must be remembered that Augustine's teaching, by the time Hilton immersed himself in it in the fourteenth century, had already undergone a number of transvaluations, not least in St Gregory the Great and St Bernard of Clairvaux. St Bernard and the Cistercians, in particular, had indelibly stamped their own personal insights and christo-centric emphases upon the framework of Augustinian spirituality.[16] Evidence of these transvaluations is met with throughout Hilton's teaching. Nevertheless the conceptual framework which may be identified with Augustine's own anagogic transvaluations of Johannine and Pauline teaching is that which underpins Hilton's own work as we shall see.

Although Hilton's major works were written after he joined the Augustinians at Thurgarton he must have been aware of the Augustinian inheritance from an earlier exposure. This raises the question of his earlier life and experience. It is now thought he had tried out the life of a solitary and had found himself unsuited to it. He tells Adam Horsley he was searching for a more active way of serving the Church.[17] The contemplative existence perhaps initiated him into the introspective element in Augustine's teaching but also made him aware of the interdependence of the active and contemplative lives in Augustine's own experience. Prior to becoming a solitary it is thought Hilton was practising as a canon lawyer. The transition from the life of lawyer to solitary and then to Augustinian suggests, perhaps, he may have had a series of compelling contemplative experiences of divine grace. The idea is purely speculative but nevertheless plausible in the light of his subsequent insights.

It is now thought that Hilton qualified as a canon lawyer at Cambridge. There is evidence he may have belonged to a group of northern clerks who were attached to the household of Thomas Arundel, Bishop of Ely, and received preferment at Peterhouse, a college which specialised in canon law.[18] It has been

---

[15] *Scale* 2, chap 21, 227 in the Clark/Dorward edition.

[16] E.J. Stormon, 'The pirituality of St Bernard' in: Noel J. Ryan (Ed.), *Christian spiritual theology*, Melbourne: Dove Communications, 1976, 150-151.

[17] Clark/Dorward edition of the *Scale*, 15.

[18] *Ibid.*, 14, 15 and n. 9. For his legal career see *Walter Hilton's Latin writings*, (ed. J.P.H. Clark & C. Taylor) Salzburg 1987, 262.

calculated, based on the average time it took to qualify and the age at which a person might begin a course at Cambridge that Hilton was born early in the thirteen forties.[19] All the evidence is circumstantial but seems plausible.

The connection with Arundel is important. As a patron he would surely have exercised influence. He was one of the central figures in the political and religious history of the period.[20] He was appointed Bishop of Ely at the age of twenty four. His youth would indicate it was a political appointment. Yet his ministry suggests he was not without a genuine vocation. In 1388 he became archbishop of York at the time of the Appellant *inter-regnum* in which development his brother Richard, the Earl of Arundel, was a protagonist. In this role he continued the work of his predecessors to upgrade the quality of the clergy, much depleted by the outbreaks of the plague in 1349 and again in 1361. While a member of his household at Ely, Hilton may have been influenced by Arundel's reform aspirations.[21]

Before Arundel was elevated to York he was also appointed Chancellor and served in this role from 1386-89 and again from 1395-96. He was briefly exiled in 1396, the year of Hilton's death, but returned to resume his career as archbishop of Canterbury. His involvement in the tortuous political manoeuvrings of Richard's reign, whatever his motives, does not seem to have diminished his desire to strengthen the Church. He was well placed to minimise the demands for access to church revenues for secular purposes, a development that had been a source of tension between Church and State at various times throughout the century. His career may have provided Hilton with an insight into the problem of how the Christian must struggle for a balance between engagement with, and disengagement from, the world of affairs. It was a problem Hilton himself experienced in his canon law practice as we have noticed. It is also reflected in the attention he devotes to the 'active' and 'contemplative' lives in the *Scale of Perfection* and the *Mixed Life* and how contemplative practise might be perfected. His works also reflect a concern with stability and tradition, especially attempts to refute Lollard teaching in which Arundel gave the lead, moving with increasing severity to eliminate Lollard preachers.[22] Hilton's presence at Thurgarton, with his canon law background, may have influenced Arundel's choice in 1388 of the Prior to examine suspected Lollard preachers.

Uncertainty also surrounds the canon of Hilton's works. The works which have been drawn upon in this study are those currently accepted as Hilton's;

---

[19] See reconstruction in my *A strange tongue* (Leuven: Peeters, 2002), 127, 128.
[20] For the relations between Church and State in Richard II's reign and Arundel's role see Peter Heath, *Church and the Realm 1272-1461*, London: Fontana Paperbacks, 1988, 189-222.
[21] Clark/Dorward editon of the *Scale*, 15.
[22] McFarlane, *John Wycliffe and the beginning of English non-conformity*, 121-159.

that is, the *Scale of Perfection*, Books I and II and the treatise on the *Mixed Life*, both written in Middle English, and four Latin treatises. A number of other works have been attributed to Hilton with varying degrees of probability.[23] Two English works, the *Angels Song* and the *Eight Chapters on Perfection*, a free translation from the Latin original by the Aragonese friar, Dom Luis de Fontibus, have a high degree of probability. Works attributed to Hilton with perhaps a lesser probability are a further Latin letter,[24] a translation into English of the *Stimulus Amoris* of the Franciscan, James of Milan,[25] and commentaries in English on the psalms, 'Qui Habitat' and 'Bonum Est' and on the 'Benedictus'.[26] Hilton's name has also been associated, erroneously, with authorship of the *Cloud of Unknowing* and the *Imitatio Christi*. Nevertheless these attributions provide some idea of the esteem with which Hilton's work was regarded.

The main source for this study is the *Scale of Perfection*.[27] In the absence of a critical edition of the work, the most accessible modern English edition, that of

---

[23]   *Eight Chapters on Perfection* and *Angels Song* translated into modern English by Rosemary Dorward, Fairacres, Oxford: S.L.G. Press, 1983. In the Translator's Preface, Rosemary Dorward comments that the *Eight Chapters on Perfection* have been found in twelve manuscripts, five of which are incomplete. The original work has not been found so it is uncertain whether the 'Eight Chapters are consecutive or how much of the original they comprise'. *Angels Song* is extant in six known manuscripts and one black-letter edition.

[24]   *Tractatus de adoratione imaginum*, (Concerning the adoration of images), (Br.Lib. MS Royal 11 Bx.f.), 178-183. It is against Wycliffe.

[25]   J.P.H. Clark. 'Action and contemplation in Walter Hilton', in: *Downside Review* 97 (1979), 268: fn.27. Doubt has been cast on the attribution of the translation to Hilton (cf. M.G. Sargent, 'A new manuscript of "the Chastising of God's Children"', in: *Medium Aevum* 46 (1977), 49ff.). In the 'Lightsome darkness: Aspects of Walter Hilton's theological background', in: *Downside Review* 95 (1977), 95: fn.3, Clark points out that Dr A.M. Hudson has informed him that the attribution to Hilton occurs in only four out of sixteen extant MSS and that of these two are certainly, and four are probably, textually related.

[26]   Clark, 'Lightsome darkness', 95, says Miss Jones in her edition of the *Minor works of Walter Hilton* (London: Burns and Oates, 1928), included the commentaries on the psalms, *Qui Habitat* and *Bonum Est* and on the *Benedictus*, on the grounds of their association with Hilton's known works in the manuscripts, but they are not explicitly ascribed to him.

[27]   A critical edition from the known MSS is in preparation, Book I edited by M.G. Sargent completing the work of the late A.J. Bliss and Book II by S.S. Hussey as noted in the Introduction to the Clark/Dorward edition of the *Scale*, 53. According to J.P.H. Clark, 'Augustine, Anselm and Walter Hilton' in *M. M. T. E.* (1982), 122: fn.48, Professor Bliss was using MS Cambridge University Library Add. 6686 for *Scale* Book I, while Professor Hussey is using British Library MS Harley 6579 for *Scale* Book II. See also reference in M.D. Knowles, *The English mystical tradition*, London: Burns and Oates, 1961, 101: fn.2. Further Clark, 'Action and contemplation in Walter Hilton', 274: fn.57, says 'A list of extant MSS kindly given me by Professor S.S. Hussey gives forty-five copies of *Scale* Book I in English and twenty-six *Scale* Book II in English; eleven Latin texts of *Scale* I and thirteen of *Scale* II are known'. In addition Hussey, 'Walter Hilton: Traditionalist', 10, points out the diversity of the manuscript tradition: 'For what the statistics are worth 19 English manuscripts – including Cambridge

Leo Sherley-Price, has been used.[28] It was a difficult choice to make because in doing so the flavour and vitality of the original Middle English is totally lost. However, most editions available include some compromise to eliminate the more difficult expressions of the Middle English.

In this discussion, we seek to examine themes which are prominent in Hilton's work and how they are integrated by the love of God, exemplified in the humanity of Christ. The themes are, the 'two lives', the contemplative process, the roles of knowledge and grace in the process, and the 'image and likeness' teaching. The discussion is focussed on the relationship between the 'love of God in Christ' orientation of Hilton's teaching and the other themes together with the pedagogic challenges which he faced in introducing those unfamiliar with it to the contemplative tradition.[29]

At the beginning of Book I of the *Scale of Perfection* the classic dichotomy of the spiritual life in its 'active' and 'contemplative' dimensions is set out. 'Love' and 'charity' are central to his definitions of both dimensions:

University Library Additonal 6686 (the base text for Book I) and the Bodley and Simeon anthologies – and two manuscripts of Latin text contain Book I alone, either in whole or in part. Only 4 manuscripts in English and only one in Latin contain Book II alone, and one manuscript, British Library Harley 330 has Book I in English but Book II in Latin. Magdalene College, Cambridge.4.17 with Book II alone in English has unique readings in Chapter 1 with the apparent purpose of removing references back to the first Book'.

[28] Leo Sherley-Price, *Ladder of P erfection*, Harmondsworth: Penguin Books, 1957, Introduction, xxiii, 'this rendering of the Ladder of Perfection is based on Dr Evelyn Underhill's edition using original manuscripts (principally B.L. Harley 6579) first published by John M. Watkins in 1923 and reprinted in 1950. This edition was the first to be made directly from early MSS sources since the book's first printing by Wynkyn de Worde in 1494, and in preparing the text Miss Underhill carefully examined ten other early versions of the work'. J.P.H. Clark in his article '*The Cloud of Unknowing*, Walter Hilton and St John of the Cross: A comparison', in: *Downside Review* 96 (1978), 281: fn.3, remarks: 'Evelyn Underhill's edition of both books was based on H (= B.L. Harley 6579) which suffices for *Scale* II (where the textual tradition is relatively simple) but not for *Scale* I where H has visible later alterations and Christo-centric additions later than Hilton. The near contemporary Latin version of both parts by Thomas Fishlake O.C. (York Minster, MS K xvi, 5 = Y) provides a check on readings'. He notes elsewhere ('Lightsome Darkness', 97), that Miss Underhill noted some, but not all, of the interpolations which are now thought by 'competent scholars' to be the work of later editors.

[29] In the case of the *Scale of Perfection* (I have preferred to use this title as most commonly used in the literature rather than Sherley-Price's translation '*Ladder of Perfection*'), an attempt has been made to understand the nature of the loss of authenticity involved in using the Sherley-Price modern English version by comparing it with Underhill's edition on which it was based and BL Harley 6579. However, the time available to me was insufficient to do more than make spot comparisons. It seems that the Sherley-Price edition is satisfactory and I am unaware of any deficiencies in it other than those inherent in the Harley 6579 manuscript itself, referred to above. References are to *Scale* 1 and *Scale* 2 in these notes. Page numbers are from the Sherley-Price edition, except where otherwise stated.

The active life consists in love and charity shown outwardly in good works, in obedience to God's commandments, and in performing the seven corporal and spiritual acts of mercy.[30]

while

the contemplative life consists in perfect love and charity inwardly experienced
through the spiritual virtues and in a true knowledge and perception of God and
spiritual things. This life belongs especially to those who for the love of God for-
sake all worldly riches, honours, and outward affairs and devote themselves body
and soul to the service of God in spiritual occupations.[31]

The contemplative life goes beyond just 'love' and 'charity' to 'perfect love and
charity'. In turn it is broken down in Book I into three degrees and, outlining
in what the third degree consists, Hilton introduces all the other major themes
of this study:

The third degree of contemplation which is the highest attainable in this life,
consists of both 'knowledge' and 'love'; that is, in knowing God and loving Him
perfectly. This is achieved when the soul is restored to the 'likeness of Jesus' and
filled with all virtues. It is then endowed with 'grace', detached from all earthly
and carnal affections, and from all unprofitable thoughts and considerations of created things, and is caught up out of its bodily senses. The 'grace' of God then illumines the mind to see all truth – that is God – and spiritual things in Him with
a soft, sweet, burning love. So perfectly is this effected that for a while the soul
becomes united to God in an ecstasy of love, and is conformed to the 'likeness of
the Trinity'. The beginning of this contemplation may be experienced in this life,
but its consummation is reserved for the bliss of heaven. Saint Paul says of this
union and conformation to our Lord: Qui adhaeret Deo, unus spiritus est cum
illo (1 Cor. VI.17). That is, whenever a soul is united to God in this ecstasy of
love, then God and the soul are no longer two but one; not indeed in nature but
in spirit. In this union a true marriage is made between God and the soul which
shall never be broken.[32]

The goal of Christian life is attained in achieving the highest degree of contemplation. Hilton reiterates the traditional view that the contemplative life is the
ideal which should be sought. It is realised when the Christian knows God and
loves him perfectly. Hilton develops the concept of the relationship between
knowledge and love with a new emphasis. In order to achieve the dual goals
which mark the highpoint of Christian desire, it is necessary for the soul to
achieve the 'likeness of Jesus' and this likeness is transformed into that of the

---

[30] *Scale* 1, 2.
[31] *Ibid.*, 3.
[32] *Ibid.*, 7.

Trinity through the working of love and grace. The role of grace is central in the achievement of the union with God which perfects the transformation to the likeness of the Trinity. So all the themes that must be explored are interrelated. The manner in which Hilton combines the themes, and places the emphasis, ultimately gives his spiritual teaching its individuality.

The Two Lives

In his definition of the two lives, Hilton acknowledged his debt to Gregory the Great; more than that he seemed to be seeking support from the authority of St Gregory.[33] However, in applying the definitions Hilton went beyond Gregory because the problem he sought to address derived from a different social situation. In Roman society it had been quite customary for men of affairs to spend their retirement in philosophic pursuits.[34] For Gregory, and even more so for St Augustine, the problem was one of apologetics, to transform a pagan custom into a Christian one, to help men find true wisdom, that is Christian wisdom.[35] But more than that, since the contemplative life was the 'better part', it was necessary to ensure that the pursuit of a religious calling did not neglect it.[36] Gregory's principal concern was to achieve a balance in the religious life between the contemplative and active aspects. Hilton's position was quite different. He had several centuries of organised contemplative life in various monastic traditions between his own time and those for which Gregory and Augustine were writing. The desire was once again emerging in some sections of the laity to pursue the contemplative life not as a pagan pursuit of philosophy, but as the ultimate wisdom, the crowning achievement of Christian endeavour. Hilton therefore seems to have been faced with the problem of adapting the rich contemplative tradition for the religious solitary, the secular clergy and the dedicated lay person. He was conscious of doing so in an intellectual climate in which *unquiet souls* were questioning doctrine.[37] Therefore

---

[33] *Ibid.*, 2.

[34] Peter Brown, *Augustine of Hippo*, London: Faber and Faber, 1967, 115, for discussion of *otium liberale* (cultured retirement), and at 145 he says, 'We meet such philosophers in some sarcophagi of the time: austere, tranquil figures, sitting among a small circle of admiring disciples, a book open on their knees – the highest human type that the classical culture of Late Antique thought could produce'.

[35] *Ibid.* The concept of *christianae vitae otium* (the peace of Christian life).

[36] Mary's was the 'better part'. See Augustine, *Sermon*, xlix.17 quoted by Butler, *Western mysticism*, 233.

[37] Kieckhefer, *Unquiet souls*, 2, 3 and J.P.H. Clark. 'Walter Hilton and the liberty of spirit', in: *Downside Review* 96 (1978).

there is a particular note of caution in his teaching. Both St Gregory and St Augustine had referred to the dichotomy of 'active' and 'contemplative' as applicable to all forms of Christian life, but primarily in the context of the religious life though by no means exclusively.[38] Hilton is equally positive. Like St Gregory he stresses that the 'active' life should precede the 'contemplative'. Of the active life he says,

> This is the life suited to all who live in the world and who enjoy wealth and ample goods. It is also suited to all who hold positions of rank, authority and responsibility over others, and who have means at their disposal whether they are learned or unlearned, laymen and churchmen: in short, all men of the world.[39]

In fact, the only exclusion from 'all men of the world' seems to be those in enclosed orders.

He goes on to explain that they are bound to execute their duties with zeal and wisdom, to give as generously as they are able and to discipline their bodies by fasting, vigils and other severe forms of penance, for the body must be chastised 'with discretion' to atone for past misdoings and make it obedient and ready to obey the spirit. 'These practices though active in form, greatly assist and dispose a person in the early stages of the spiritual life to approach the contemplative life'.[40]

The contemplative life follows the active life which has to achieve a certain quality as a *sine qua non* to entering upon the contemplative phase. For Gregory the active and contemplative lives were interchangeable; the prelate spent part of his day in the service of his 'neighbour' and part in contemplation. For Hilton there is a continuum; reformation has to occur before contemplation can be achieved. He is thinking of people in the early stages of the spiritual life. But Hilton is not ruling out the possibility of the lay person approaching the contemplative life.

In Book I of the *Scale* he outlines three degrees of contemplation which follow traditional teaching, with the exception that the second stage is divided into two parts.[41] This subdivision seems to cater for the layman, but not exclusively.

The first stage of the second degree of contemplation consists principally in loving God and does not depend upon intellectual light in spiritual matters.[42] Consequently it is usually attained 'by simple and unlearned folk who give themselves completely to devotion'.[43] It is characterised by feelings of love and spiri-

---

[38] Butler, *Western mysticism*, 157-191.
[39] *Scale* 1, 2.
[40] *Ibid.*
[41] *Ibid.*, chaps. 4-9.
[42] *Scale* 1, 5.
[43] *Ibid.*

tual fervour, great trust in the goodness and mercy of God, heartfelt fear and awe; by joy, delight and comfort – 'sweet tears scour and cleanse the soul from all stains of sin and cause it to melt with wonderful love for Jesus Christ (...) whoever has [these feelings] is in Charity',[44] by which he means is experiencing the love of God.

The higher stages of this second degree of contemplation are less demonstratively affective. They are reached by those who have attained 'great peace of body and soul and who by the grace of Jesus Christ and through prolonged bodily and spiritual discipline have found peace of heart and purity of conscience, so that they desire nothing more than live quietly in constant prayer to God, and in meditation on our Lord'.[45]

The first stage of this degree of contemplation is more easily reached than the second, which is characterised more by the desire for God's love than the enjoyment of it. Those in this state wait in prayerful expectation but an expectation which is not made unquiet by any doubt. Hilton, when comparing this degree of contemplation with the third, makes the distinction between love on fire with devotion'[46] compared with the third when love is 'on fire with contemplation':

> God gives this degree of contemplation where He will, both to learned and to simple, to men and women in spiritual authority, and to solitaries; but it is an especial favour, and not common. And although a person living the active life may receive this gift as an especial favour, none but a contemplative or solitary can possess it in all its fullness.[47]

Hilton will not exclude the lay person from the third degree of contemplation but he does not think the layman has a great chance of achieving it. The two stages of the second degree seem to be the most that the lay person could expect and then the second stage is rarely to be achieved either. The first stage he seems to regard as more commonly achievable, but it is also dependent on God's grace. In his *Epistola de Utilitate et Prerogativis Religionis* (On the Usefulness and Prerogatives of Religion) he develops his ideas of the relationship between the lay and religious lives further:

> [I]n the body of Christ, the Church, not all the members have the same work, for one sees in contemplation, another hears in obedience, another eagerly tastes the sweetness of devotion, another touches through the bodily performance of the commandments of God.[48]

---

[44] *Ibid.*, 5, 6.
[45] *Ibid.*, 6, 7.
[46] *Ibid.*, chap.9, 8.
[47] *Ibid.*, chap.9, 9.
[48] Quoted by J. Russell-Smith in 'Walter Hilton', in: James Walsh (Ed.), *Pre-reformation English spirituality*, New York: Fordham University Press, 1965, 182. The source is MS. Bod.Lat. th. e 26, fol.l30.

In other words, God's call is not the same for everyone; there are many diverse calls within the Church. Moreover, the lay person who follows his vocation faithfully will receive the same rewards as a religious. *In the Epistola ad Quemdam Saeculo Renunciare Volentem* (Letter to Someone Wanting to Renounce the World), he teaches:

> Certainly God has his own, whether beginning, proficient or perfect, outside regular religion as well as in. For just as those in religion who fulfil their profession as fully as the great frailty of our modern times permits can attain the perfection of charity by God's gift, through exercising the virtues of obedience, chastity and voluntary poverty, so outside regular religion, if any person for love of Christ turns from love of the world and all its concerns and preoccupations (at least in the whole direction of his mind) and chooses poverty, steady prayer, and continued meditation, and devotes himself to the other virtues as whole-heartedly as human frailty allows, certainly he may aspire to the same fulness of charity and spiritual gifts through the grace of Christ as he might if he had entered religion.[49]

Indeed he might do better than the religious:

> Some man or woman of the world, lord or lady, knight or squire, merchant or ploughman will have a higher reward than some priest or friar, monk or canon, or enclosed anchoress. And why? Surely because he has a greater love for God.[50]

The core of his teaching is expressed in the first chapter of the *Mixed Life*. It is based on the text *ordinavit in me caritatem* (he has planted charity within me):

> Thou shalt not utterly follow thy desire to leave occupation and business of the world (which are needful to use in ruling thyself and of all others that are under thy keeping) and give thee wholly to ghostly occupations of prayers and meditations, as it were a friar, or a monk or another man that were not bounden to the world by children and servants as thou art; for it falleth not to thee, and if thou do so thou keepest not the order of Charity. Also if you wouldest leave utterly ghostly occupation – especially now after the grace that God hath given unto thee – and set thee wholly to the business of the world in fulfilling works of active life, as fully as another man that never felt devotion, thou leavest the order of Charity.[51]

---

[49] Quoted by Russell-Smith, 'Walter Hilton', 183.The source is MS. B.L. Royal 6 E III fol.119 r.a. Translation is her own.

[50] *Scale* 1, 75.

[51] Quoted by Russell-Smith, 'Walter Hilton', 184. The source is Hilton's *Mixed Life* in *Minor works of Walter Hilton* (ed. D. Jones), London: Burns, Oates & Washbourne, 1929. Joy Russell-Smith, says 'minor modernisations have occasionally been introduced' (p. 182, fn.2).

Hilton poses the dilemma for the devout layman. On the one hand he cannot abandon his worldly responsibilities; on the other, he must cooperate with the special graces of devotion he has been given, as fully as he can. He may never achieve full worldly success nor can he give his undivided attention to the pursuit of the perfect love which is the goal of the spiritual life. It is a dilemma with which St Augustine and St Gregory and, no doubt Walter Hilton, were well acquainted in their religious vocation also.[52]

Hilton's advice is not to be over-scrupulous:

> [A]nd therefore when thou doest a good deed or prayest or thinkest on God, think not in thine heart, doubting whether thou desirest or not; for thy deed showest thy desire.[53]

Nevertheless he is careful to avoid the imputation that the active life is the better part:

> [T]herefore when thou prayest or thinkest on God thy desire to God is more whole, more fervent and more ghostly than when thou doest other outward good deeds unto thy even-Christian.[54]

This is the crux, he commends the 'Mixed Life' of which Christ's life is the example:

> I hold this life middled best and most behoveful to them as long as they are bounden thereto.[55]

Hilton is extending St Gregory's concept of the necessary balance between the active and contemplative aspects in the religious life to the devout lay person. But he is in no sense advocating religious egalitarianism. The lay person who pursues the contemplative life needs direction:

> I speak of those seculars who do not fear to set out on the way of the spiritual life without a director or capable guide, whether man or book, obeying their own impulse.[56]

Hilton set out to provide the direction in cautious but helpful and forward-looking terms.

---

[52] Both lament the difficulty of extracting themselves from the cares of office.
[53] Hilton, *Mixed life*, 49, 50. Quoted by Russell-Smith, 'Walter Hilton', 185.
[54] *Ibid.*, 52.
[55] *Ibid.* Quoted by Russell-Smith, 'Walter Hilton', 186.
[56] Letter to Adam Horsley on the religious state is quoted by Russell-Smith, 'Walter Hilton', 193. The source is Bod. Lat. th. e.26. fol.127. Russell-Smith's translation.

The Contemplative Process

It has been argued convincingly by Joy Russell-Smith, and the view is supported by Professor S. S. Hussey, that although Book II of the *Scale* was genuinely an extension of Book I, it was also intended for a wider audience than the anchoress to whom Book I had been addressed.[57] She suggests that it may have been intended as a guide for spiritual directors. This interpretation is consistent with the change in the profundity of the discussion which is probably the most important difference between the two books of the *Scale*.[58] In Book I Hilton provides a broad summary of traditional teaching on the active and contemplative lives and the three degrees of contemplation, developing particularly the analysis of the process by which the soul is purged of sin. In Book II he introduces his own unique insights into the contemplative process, the dichotomy between 'reformation in faith' and 'reformation in faith and feeling' and the concept of the 'lightsome darkness' which it seems necessary to experience before the 'reformation in faith' can be transposed to reformation in both faith and feeling. Book I provides the introduction to the purgation process which is the prerequisite of reformation.

The Reverend J.P.H. Clark in a series of most interesting articles has analysed the theology and the theological roots of Hilton's ideas of the two-stage reformation process and the 'lightsome darkness'.[59] The principle concern in this study is to examine the concept of the love of God in the humanity of Christ in Hilton's thinking. He begins his analysis of the role of love in the following way:

> [T]he love of God has three degrees (...) The first degree is reached by faith alone, when no knowledge of God is conveyed by grace through the imagination or understanding (...) The second degree of love is attained when the soul knows God by faith and Jesus in His manhood through the imagination (...) In the third degree the soul as far as it may in this life, contemplates the Godhead united

---

[57] Russell-Smith, 'Walter Hilton', 188-190 and Hussey, 'Walter Hilton: Traditionalist', 10.

[58] It has also been argued that Book 2 of the *Scale* was written some years after Book 1 and the difference in the level of discussion attributed to greater experience and maturity as well as a different purpose. In Book I, for example, Hilton acknowledges references to St Augustine on six occasions, St Gregory on four and St Bernard on two, as if he was seeking the support of their authority for his views. In Book 2 there are no special acknowledgements and no references to Hilton's personal inexperience in the spiritual life. It has a much more confident tone about it. On the differences between Books I and 2 of the *Scale*, see Russell-Smith, 'Walter Hilton', 187-190 and also Helen Gardner ('The text of the *Scale of Perfection*', in: *Medium Aevum* 5 (1936), 14-15), and Gerard Sitwell, 'Contemplation in the *Scale of Perfection*', in: *Downside Review* 67 (1949), 277.

[59] Clark. 'Augustine, Anselm and Walter Hilton', 102-126. Also 'Lightsome Darkness', 95-109. Also 'The *Cloud Of Unknowing*, Walter Hilton and St John of the Cross', 281-298.

to manhood in Christ. This is the best, the highest and most perfect degree of love, and it is not attained by the soul until it is reformed in feeling. Those at the beginning and early stages of the spiritual life do not possess this degree of love, for they cannot think of Jesus or love Him as God but always think of Him as man living under earthly conditions.[60]

The three degrees of love parallel the three degrees of contemplation encountered in Book I of the *Scale*. The first degree of love is only touched on in Book II but in Book I Hilton echoes St Gregory. To become a contemplative,

> You must begin at the beginning and there are three things which you need as a secure foundation; these are humility, firm faith and a whole-hearted intention towards God.[61]

He further defines a 'whole-hearted intention' as: '[A] sincere resolve and desire to please God. For this is love, without which all your efforts are valueless'.[62]

As the soul progresses towards achieving a likeness of Jesus, a key concept to be dealt with later, through grace and an increasing knowledge of Christ in his humanity, so the soul attains the second degree of love. It is the transformation from the second to the third degree of love that interests Hilton in Book II. To make the transformation the soul has to experience the 'darkness':

> [D]eath to the world is this darkness; it is the gateway to contemplation and reformation in feeling. There is no other way (…) it leads (…) to self-knowledge and humility and mortifies all love of the world so that he [the soul] can sometimes feel himself deep in this peaceful darkness where he is hidden from the vanity of the world.[63]

And again:

> [The experience of darkness] consists firstly in self-knowledge, deep peace, and then self-transcendence through a burning desire to see Jesus; or more accurately the experience is itself a spiritual perception of Jesus.[64]

That spiritual perception of Jesus is the realisation that Jesus is in fact the triune God:

> The soul does not know God as He is, for no creature in heaven or earth can do this… But it recognises Him as changeless being, as sovereign power, sovereign truth and sovereign goodness, and as the source of blessing, life and eternal bliss.

---

[60] *Scale* 2, 188.
[61] *Scale* 1, 16.
[62] *Ibid.*, 25. Similar images used by St Gregory.
[63] *Scale* 2, 177.
[64] *Ibid.*, 175.

The soul perceives these truths and many others, but not as bare, abstract, savour-
less theory (…) understanding is uplifted by the grace of the Holy Spirit and illumined (…) with wondering reverence, ardent love, spiritual delight and heavenly
joy.[65]

and

[F]or a soul that has experienced a little of this union with Jesus [can do nothing
other than] devote itself entirely to obtaining a clearer knowledge and deeper love
of Jesus, and in Him of all the Blessed Trinity…[66]

He sums up:

This opening of the eyes of the soul to the knowledge of the Godhead I call
reform in faith and feeling. For the soul has some experience of what it once
knew by faith alone.[67]

The first point is that Hilton, in common with traditional teaching, expresses
the central paradox of Christian spirituality. On the one hand there is the awareness of a union with Jesus and of the reality of experiencing both Jesus and the
Triune Godhead; on the other that this awareness is incomplete. The experience
is so compelling that it drives the soul to seek a clearer knowledge and a deeper
love.

In passing it is worth noting that there are distinct similarities between Hilton's
understanding of the ultimate phases of the contemplative process and the ideas
of William of St Thierry about *unitas spiritus* and *amor intellectus est*.

Hilton is only too conscious of the difficulty of articulating the experience.
The mystery and difficulty is expressed in the following passage:

This opening of the spiritual eyes is that glowing darkness and rich nothingness
of which I spoke earlier. It may be called: 'Purity of soul and spiritual rest, inward
stillness and peace of conscience, refinement of thought and integrity of soul, a
lively consciousness of grace and solitude of heart, the wakeful sleep of the spouse
and the tasting of heavenly joys, the ardour of love and brightness of light, the
entry into contemplation and reformation in feeling'. All these terms are employed
by various writers in spiritual literature, for each of them spoke of his own experience of grace; and although they use different expressions they are all speaking
of the same truth.[68]

'The glowing darkness and rich nothingness' as Sherley-Price has translated the
notion of 'lightsome darkness' is the image which Hilton has chosen to express

---

[65] *Ibid.*, 195, 196.
[66] *Ibid.*, 198.
[67] *Ibid.*, 200.
[68] *Ibid.*, 223.

the paradox of 'incomplete awareness'. As J.P.H. Clark has pointed out this is not the apophatic night which is central to the pseudo-Dionysian concept.[69]

The awareness derives from a combination of knowledge and love and this is because 'God is love'. The following passages illustrate the point:

> [T]he ultimate joy and end of the soul depends upon this knowledge of God, you may perhaps wonder why I said earlier that the soul should desire nothing but the love of God, yet said nothing about the nature of the soul's desire for this knowledge. My answer is that knowledge of God brings perfect happiness to the soul and that this happiness derives not only from knowledge, but the blessed love which springs from it. Nevertheless love derives from knowledge and not knowledge from love; consequently the happiness of the soul is said to derive chiefly from this knowledge and experience of God to which is conjoined the love of God. And the better God is known the more He is loved.[70]

and

> God Himself is both the means by which the soul attains this knowledge and the love that derives from it.[71]

and again,

> [T]he saints say (…) that there are two kinds of spiritual love, uncreated love and created (…) uncreated love is God Himself, the third person of the Trinity, that is, the Holy Spirit. He is love uncreated as St John says: 'Deus dilectio est' (1 John IV.8) (…) Created love is love implanted and aroused in a soul by the Holy Spirit when it sees and knows Truth, that is God (…) it is brought into being by the Holy Spirit (…) He gives up His love, that is the Holy Spirit. He is both the Giver and the Gift and by that Gift He makes us know and love Him. This is the Divine Love which I said should be the sole object of your desire, the uncreated love that is the Holy Spirit.[72]

---

[69] Clark, 'The lightsome darkness', 98:
'Hilton's use of 'darkness' has no apophatic overtones at all. It refers not to the 'darkness' that impinges on us through the ontological transcendence of God, through the excess of his light (…) but to the darkness within man himself in his fallen condition'. While the 'fallen condition' interpretation is borne out in other contexts within the *Scale*, in the context from which this quotation is taken, it clearly refers to the 'opening of the spiritual eyes'. Self- knowledge, of course, reveals the 'image of sin' in the soul and this, as Hilton tells us is a necessary pre-condition for the opening of the spiritual eyes and for reformation to the 'Likeness of Jesus'. There is a remarkable harmonic with the idea expressed by St Gregory the Great in *Morals* v.53: 'She [the soul] thoroughly discovers herself guilty in proportion as she sees herself to have been out of harmony with the light which shines in the midst of darkness above her...'

[70] *Scale* 2, 201.

[71] *Ibid.*, 202.

[72] *Ibid.*, 202. Hussey in 'Walter Hilton: Traditionalist' (p. 11) suggests that the source of Hilton's description of God as both 'Giver and the Gift' may be St Bernard's *De Diligendo Deo*:

Hilton is perhaps suggesting in these passages that love of God is the forerunner of knowledge of God. However, love does not necessarily lead to knowledge, in the experiential sense, whereas knowledge always brings with it love. Two ideas are implicit in this suggestion. First grace, through the presence of the Holy Spirit within the soul (the Gift), arouses love which is understood by faith and this is the key which starts and maintains the process of reformation in faith. But, second, when God reveals Himself through Jesus in that 'lightsome darkness' He is known by experience and loved because of that knowledge. This is the watershed experience which Hilton calls 'reformation of faith and feeling'. The ecstatic experience is brief but having once experienced it, its power is transforming, 'uniting God and the Soul in a single will'.[73] The virtuous life becomes easy because the soul 'reformed in faith and feeling' desires nothing more than to do God's will.

The insights into the contemplative process which Hilton provides in his descriptions of the transposition of the three degrees of contemplation of Book I of the *Scale*, into 'reformation in faith' and to 'reformation in faith and feeling' in Book II have a close parallel in John Burnaby's analysis of St Augustine's idea and exposition of the contemplative process:

> The form of this 'inchoate contemplation' is that very search for God of which so many of Augustine's writings, and above all the second parts of the Confessions and the De Trinitate, provide examples. The method has been well described by the Augustinian Father Fulbert Cayré. It is 'through an intellectual discipline, mystical in tendency, to lift the reader, little by little, to that spiritual state which is the indispensible condition of the fuller enlightenment'. The aim is not to demonstrate theological propositions, but to show God, to bring Him into the heart so that He may be felt. So much Augustine did believe to be possible, and possible for all: the Confessions at least, he did not write for an intellectual elite. And such separate acts of 'contemplative meditation', such liftings of the heart to God, are to be the pattern for the gradual day-by-day renewal or restoration of the divine image in the soul, grace working for the perfection of nature.[74]

For Augustine as for Walter Hilton the search for God was an extended process; not so much a process of, at least, partial intellectual revelation, although this

---

'He is both prime mover of our love and final end. He is Himself our human soul's occasion; He also gives the power of love, and brings desire to its consummation. He is Himself the Loveable in His essential Being, and gives Himself to be the Object of our love (…) He gave Himself to be our Righteousness, and keeps Himself to be our great reward'. Translated as *On the Love of God* by a religious of the Community of St Mary the Virgin (London and Oxford: Mowbray, 1950), 53.

[73] *Scale* 2, 225.

[74] J. Burnaby, *Amor Dei*, London: Hodder & Stoughton, 1938, 68.

may be a by-product, but a process of conditioning and experiencing that He might be felt in the soul.

Knowledge of God

The 'conjoining' of knowledge with love is a key feature, as has been shown, of Hilton's idea of reformation in 'faith and feeling'. His emphasis on knowledge of God should, perhaps, be further investigated, for, *prima facie*, it appears to conflict with the view that distrust of the speculative, and academic, is a tradition of English spirituality. But the conflict may be more apparent than real;

> We should have deep desire for this experience [contemplation] for every rational soul should desire with all its strength to draw close to God and to be united to Him by its awareness of His unseen presence. It is easier to attain knowledge of this presence by personal experience than by reading books, for it is life and love, strength and light, joy and peace to a chosen soul.[75]

He is not so much disparaging 'book' learning in this passage as saying that there is no substitute for the personal experience of God's presence in the soul. Words cannot adequately express the happiness which 'feeling' this presence brings.[76]

Hilton's mistrust of the pursuit of knowledge, particularly in theological matters, reflects in some measure the tension, which unsettled times seem to exacerbate, between faith and reason: 'By itself, knowledge is like water tasteless and cold'.[77] However, God will turn the water into wine if his aid is sought:

> He will turn this savourless knowledge into wisdom and cold naked reason into spiritual light and burning love by the gift of the Holy Spirit.[78]

He quotes the Pauline dictum '*Scientia inflat, caritas autem aedificat*' ('Knowledge inflates but charity establishes'). Learning uninformed by charity can be dangerous:

> Some people who possess this knowledge become proud and misuse it in order to increase their personal reputation, worldly rank, honours and riches, when they should use it humbly to the praise of God and for the benefit of fellow Christians in true charity. Some fall into heresies, errors and other public sins, through which they become a scandal both to themselves and to the whole church.[79]

---

[75] *Scale* 2, 233.
[76] It has already been noted that Hilton suggested that seculars who wished to pursue the contemplative life should at least seek guidance from a 'book'.
[77] *Scale* 1, 4.
[78] *Ibid.*, 5.
[79] *Ibid.*, 4.

The concern Hilton shows for orthodoxy and his respect for the Church as the repository of orthodoxy, are no doubt reinforced by the experience of his own time and his own Prior at Thurgarton. But the roots go deeper: 'The feet of knowledge are lamed by sin'.[80]

He reiterates the passage in Isaiah, which St Augustine highlighted for all future ages, '*Nisi credderitis, non intelligetis*' (unless you first believe, you cannot understand).[81] Belief comes first and understanding follows. Understanding which has been purified and enlightened by the grace of the Holy Spirit to see Truth. Without this grace the conclusions of reason are suspect, because they may be misdirected by sin-tarnished and wilful intentions.

J.P.H. Clark has made an interesting comparison of the use of the dictum from Isaiah by Augustine, St Anselm, St Bernard and Hilton.[82] For Augustine, it is used with apologetic purpose; the receptive attitude of faith is the prerequisite to becoming a Christian. For Anselm the formula is a declaration of his own faith; he seeks a rational insight into the content of revelation which he has always accepted. St Bernard's imagery creates a different nuance. He speaks of the 'flesh' of Christ as the 'shadow' under which divinity is known under conditions of this life:

> That is a good shadow of faith, which tempers the light to the clouded eye, and prepares the eye for the light: for it is written, "Purifying their hearts by faith".[83]

For Hilton also reformation in faith comes first and it is followed by reformation in 'feeling'. As Clark suggests 'feeling' is a term which embraces both knowledge and love, not only understanding but also affection. Above all, however, it encompasses 'a supernaturally given awareness of the life of grace'.

> This tasting of manna is a lively consciousness of grace which is due to the quickening of the soul's spiritual vision.[84]

Hilton is not only in the English tradition but in the tradition of the Church; the Holy Spirit is the means by which the soul comes to faith and the power by which faith is transformed into 'Wisdom'.

---

[80] *Ibid.*, 31.
[81] *Scale* 2, 134.
[82] Clark, 'Augustine, Anselm and Walter Hilton', 106-108.
[83] *Ibid.*, 122: fn.40. St Bernard, *super Cantica canticorum* 31 3.8-4.9, in: *Bernardi Opera* (Ed. J. Leclerq, C.H. Talbot, & H.M. Rochais), Rome 1957, vol.1, 224ff.
[84] *Scale* 2, 227.

Grace

For Hilton, then, 'reformation in feeling' is above all an experience of the grace of God working within the soul. The role of grace is paramount in both stages of the reforming process but there is a distinction.[85] The early stages of contemplation are 'not accompanied by feelings of devotion infused by the special gift of the Holy Spirit'; the role of grace is accepted by faith: '…since foregiveness comes spiritually and invisibly by the grace of the Holy Spirit. He [Jesus] did not tell the man to see or feel that his sins were forgiven, but to believe',[86] and 'But some people are so worldly-minded and stupid they would like to feel, hear or see forgiveness of their sins in the same way as they feel or see a material object'.[87]

Nevertheless the soul must be prepared to receive grace. The purpose of prayer is to 'make you ready to receive grace, for although prayer is not the cause for which our Lord gives grace, it is nevertheless the means by which grace, freely given, comes to the soul'.[88]

He poses the question:

> Why should I undertake bodily penance in order to win this grace when it cannot be obtained except by the free gift of grace?[89]

and provides the answer; the person who, 'deliberately chooses worldly idleness (…) renders himself incapable of receiving the gift of grace'.[90] The soul cannot stand still, it must either grow in grace or relapse into sin.[91] In other words, the Christians must put their trust in God's promises, live and act in faith and believe that God will give whatever grace is necessary:

> We ourselves do nothing more than allow Him to act as He wills, for the most that we can do is to yield ourselves readily to the working of His grace. Yet even this readiness does not originate in us, but in Him, so that all good that we do is due to Him, although we do not realise this.[92]

The grace the soul receives is what is necessary:

---

[85] Russell-Smith, 'Walter Hilton', 191. Of the *Scale* she writes: 'The whole treatise is a coherent, comprehensive account of the supernatural life at all its stages, including the greatest experience of contemplation, with a very careful study of grace and its absence and increase'.
[86] *Scale* 2, 134.
[87] *Ibid.*
[88] *Scale* 1, 28.
[89] *Scale* 2, 154.
[90] *Ibid.*
[91] *Ibid.*, 148.
[92] *Ibid.*, 205.

No-one is suddenly endowed with all graces but when God, the source of all grace, helps and teaches a soul it can attain this state by sustained spiritual exercises and wisely ordered activity.[93]

For example, the second degree of prayer is 'never offered without some reward of grace'.[94]

There is no special way to attain the grace of perfection: 'It depends chiefly on the grace of our Lord Jesus and upon great personal efforts'.[95] There is never any mistaking this grace:

> For whenever grace comes powerfully it imposes a great strain on the spirit even while it brings joy (...) often also a great strain on the body (...) This is one effect of passionate love (...) in its violence it destroys all love of earthly things (...) wounds the soul with the sword of joyful love (...) so potent is God's touch in the soul [the soul needs] to be touched only once by his sharp sword.[96]

The experience brings about that union which produces the reformation in feeling: 'a soul (...) touched by the especial grace of the Holy Spirit (...) is uplifted (...) to a different level of experience.[97]

'The Image and Likeness' theme

Hilton's idea of 'reformation' is set in the traditional framework. The purpose of Book II of the *Scale* is to 'tell (...) how man's soul may be, and is, reformed in the likeness of Him who first created it'.[98]

The assumptions on which the development of this reformation process is based are most fully explained in Book I:

> The soul of man is a life consisting of three powers, memory, understanding and will. It is made in the image and likeness of the blessed Trinity, whole, perfect and righteous. For the mind was created strong and steadfast by virtue of the Father, so that it might hold fast to Him, neither forgetting Him, nor being distracted and hindered by created things; and so it has the likeness of the Father. The understanding was made clear and bright, without error or obscurity, and as perfect as might be in a body not glorified; and so it has the likeness of the Son, who is eternal wisdom. The will and its affections was made pure, rising like a flame towards God without love of the flesh or any creatures, by the sovereign good-

---

93 *Ibid.*, 146.
94 *Scale* 1, 38.
95 *Scale* 2, 151.
96 *Scale* 1, 33.
97 *Scale* 2, 223.
98 *Ibid.*, 114.

ness of God, the Holy Spirit; and so it has the likeness of the Holy Spirit, who
is holy love. So mans soul may be called a created trinity, was made complete in
the mind, sight and love of the uncreated and blessed Trinity, who is God. This
is the dignity and honourable state natural to man's soul at its creation.[99]

The effect of 'Original Sin' was that humankind, 'fell from that blessed Trinity
(...) into forgetfulness and ignorance of God and into a debasing and deliber-
ate love of himself'.[100]

The task of the Christian now is that, 'we should desire to recover some degree
and likeness of that dignity, so that the soul may be reformed by grace to a
shadow of the image of the Trinity which it once had by nature and which it
will have fully in heaven. This is the true life of contemplation'.[101]

These assumptions reflect ultimately St Augustine's teaching in *De Trinitate*.
However, the process by which the restoration of the likeness is achieved, is
adapted to focus on the humanity of Christ as the exemplar of what that likeness should be. In the first stage of reformation the emphasis is placed on restoring the likeness of Jesus in his humanity; in the second to the likeness of the
Blessed Trinity:

> Humility and Charity will fashion you to the likeness of Jesus in his Humanity,
> and will at length transform you to the true likeness of Jesus in his Godhead.[102]

To bring 'virtue to perfection'[103] is to follow the example of Jesus 'to be clothed
in his likeness – that is, in humility and charity which are his livery'.[104]

To achieve this likeness of Jesus is a prerequisite for further progress:

> For as long as He does not find His likeness re-formed in you He remains a
> stranger and far distant from you.[105]

He uses St Augustine's method of introversion to examine the soul. In the
absence of virtue self-examination reveals nothing,

> ... but a dark and painful image of your own soul, which has neither the light of
> the knowledge of God, nor any love and devotion to Him. This image, if you
> examine it carefully, is entirely enveloped in the black cloak of sin – pride, anger,
> spiritual indolence, covetousness, gluttony and lust (...) This is not the image of
> Jesus, but the image of sin (...) You are beginning to wonder what this image is

---

[99] *Scale* 1, 50.
[100] *Ibid.*, 50.
[101] *Ibid.*, 55.
[102] *Ibid.*, 109.
[103] *Ibid.*, 9.
[104] *Ibid.*, 62.
[105] *Ibid.*, 62.

like [of sin]; and lest you should remain long in doubt, let me tell you it is nothing material (…) In reality it is nothing (…) This 'nothing' is none else than
darkness of the mind and lack of love and light, just as sin is nothing other than
lack of God,[106]

and if this concept should prove difficult to understand,

> how I can rightly say that nothing can be an image – since nothing always remains
> nothing – I will try to elucidate my meaning. This image is false and misguided
> love of self. From this love spring all kinds of sin.[107]

The love of self is deeply rooted. As already noted it is the 'Original Sin'. To root
it out is a long and painful process.[108] The virtues of humility and charity are
the antithesis of self- love, just as the image of Jesus is the antithesis of the image
of sin. Hilton makes no bones about it – reformation means complete transformation. Until the soul is purified the second stage of the reformation will not
be experienced. And when with God's help this reformation is accomplished
much vigilance is required.

> I think it possible that a soul which is reformed in feeling and transported by love
> into the contemplation of God may be so remote from the influence of the senses
> and vain imagination and temporarily so withdrawn from physical influences that
> it is conscious of nothing but God; but this condition is not permanent. I repeat
> that everyone must fight against this sinful image, and in particular any who is
> reformed only in faith, for he may easily be deceived by it.[109]

The view of humanity which underlies Hilton's use of the 'Image and Likeness'
theme seems to be based on St Paul's teaching as interpreted and extended by
St Augustine in *De Trinitate*. The doctrine establishes the dignity of human being
as *capax Dei*; it is a potential dignity because the image has been debased. The
whole purpose of Christian life is to restore the potentiality and realise it as far
as can be in this life. St Augustine provides the theological leitmotiv in Hilton's
teaching. However Hilton, the teacher and spiritual director, is primarily concerned with the process by which restoration of the likeness is to be achieved.
In this emphasis, he follows William of St Thierry and St Bernard. He uses
St Augustine's method of introversion to examine the condition of the soul and
the image it presents but to effect its reformation, he focusses on the humanity

---

[106] *Ibid.*, 63. In this context the antithesis between light and darkness illustrates Clark's interpretation of darkness as the 'image of sin which is nothing other than lack of God'.

[107] *Ibid.*, 66.

[108] *Scale* 2, 211. Those who have the common amount of charity 'must struggle and strive all day
against their sins (…) Like wrestlers, they are sometimes on top and sometimes underneath' –
an image that was used by St Gregory.

[109] *Ibid.*, 132.

of Jesus, as the example of humility and charity in contradistinction to the 'teaching' of Jesus or Jesus as the 'Word'. It is meditation on the extent of this humility and charity which brings compunction and sorrow and enkindles the desire for reformation, and ultimately the love on which restoration of the likeness depends.

Reflection

This study has examined the main themes of Walter Hilton's teaching in the context of the centrality of the ideas of love and charity in his notion of the spiritual life. It was noted at the outset that his teaching was directed towards both secular and religious and that in particular he extended the notions of the contemplative and active dichotomy which had been applied traditionally to persons in the religious rather than secular life, to cover both classes. It has been suggested that this development in the application of a traditional concept was brought about in response to, in particular, the need to help lay people who wished to pursue the contemplative life.

The adaptations which Hilton made did not alter the traditional interpretation of the two lives. It has been suggested, on the other hand, that his refinement of the teaching on the second degree of contemplation by dividing it into two stages, perhaps, was brought about by the need to provide the simple and unlearned with a spiritual goal which would enrich their spiritual life. The use of the vernacular in the *Mixed Life* and the *Scale of Perfection* was possibly also motivated by Hilton's desire to make the imagery and beauty of traditional teaching accessible to the unlearned. The unlearned may not indeed have been able to read such works for themselves, but it did enable spiritual directors and the more educated parish clergy to express the teaching in a more readily understood idiom.

The emphasis which Hilton's teaching placed on the 'Humanity of Christ' was well suited to a lay audience without theological background. The concentration on the devotion to the humanity of Christ, the identification with his suffering and the reason for it, had been one of the main factors since the twelfth century in awakening a lay and unlearned desire for greater participation in contemplative practices. The life of Christ was a mixed life; at every turn his teaching was unfolded in contacts with the lay person, as often as not the simple and unlearned. The imagery which such contacts produced was the ideal vehicle for spiritual teaching. Even the difficult concept of the transformation of human love to spiritual love is bridged by emphasising 'the spiritual perception of Jesus' of 'feeling' Him working in the soul, through the Holy Spirit as the triune God. The mystery of the Trinity is not emphasised as a theological puzzle but as an extension of the materiality of Jesus' humanity to an unseen, but felt, presence.

Humility and charity are emphasised as the 'livery of Jesus', a metaphor which would evoke, perhaps, a rather conservative image in communities which were familiar with the causes and aftermath of the 'Peasants Revolt' of 1381. They would also evoke an image which contrasted the humble and caring bearing of Christ with the, perhaps, overbearing and grasping behaviour of some of the seigneurial class. This is not to suggest some revolutionary intent in Hilton's use of that particular contemporary image. On the contrary his teaching emphasises discipline in the practice of the virtues of humility and charity as the key to a deeper spiritual relationship.

Hilton's understanding of the spiritual life is of a growth in love. The initial step of faith is to trust. Love grows as the image of sin is recognised and wrestled with. It would be wrong to emphasise exclusively the severe ascetic orientation of Hilton's teaching, even if tempered, as indeed it is, with practical good sense, without also emphasising the growth in love which is the concomitant. Love arouses the compassion and compunction which accompanies the awareness of sin. The desire to purify the soul and destroy the image of sin is beautifully drawn by Hilton in his image of the pilgrimage to Jerusalem[110] with all the cadences of Jesus' life with which it is associated.

Despite the simplicity of Hilton's teaching about progress in the spiritual life, the profound theological roots of that teaching are evident. There is evidence of the underlying theological tensions between faith and reason, between the roles of knowledge and love, and between grace and freedom of will. In theological terms Hilton is a traditionalist. The roots of his theology are locked in the Augustinian synthesis of Pauline and Johannine teaching.

His theology of the 'Image and Likeness', uses the Augustinian framework to explain human destiny. Necessarily, the decisive influence of 'Original Sin' in defacing the image of the Trinity, in which the soul was created, underlies the human dilemma and makes the restoration process such a dour struggle. Sin is deep-rooted in human consciousness; to uproot it entirely requires the perseverance of a Saint and this explains, in part, why so few attain the heights of contemplation.[111]

---

[110] *Ibid.*, 154 ff. 'I will use the simile of a good pilgrim. A man once wished to go to Jerusalem and since he did not know the way, he called another man who, he hoped, knew the way, and asked him for information'.

[111] Russell-Smith, 'Walter Hilton', 188. In her view, the second treatise of the *Scale* is important because it illustrates why so few come to full experience of contemplation. In *Scale* 2, 147, Hilton poses the problem: 'You may say that since our Lord is so good and gracious and bestows His gifts so freely, it is surprising that so few souls come to be reformed in feeling, compared with the vast number who do not'. One reason is, 'many who have been reformed in faith do not make a wholehearted effort to grow in grace (…) they are content with the lowest place in heaven'. He goes on 149: 'But the service of God is the noblest of all crafts. It demands the greatest skill, and it is the highest and hardest in which to attain perfection'.

The ascetic problem for the Christian has its rationale in the need to convert self-love into love of God. This objective can only be accomplished with the assistance of divine grace. The theology of grace, the gift of divine love, is closely related to Hilton's devotion to the Humanity of Christ; God is both the Giver and the Gift. The love of God which brought about the creation is God Himself. This is not the pantheistic notion that God is substantially in his creation, but rather that the power by which the act of creation was begun and is maintained, is God and that power is love. God's will is God's love. When the human soul is reformed in faith and feeling, it is momentarily united to God and the two wills become one in so far as the reformed soul desires to do only God's will. The union is not in substance but results from the revelation, rather than just the visitation, of the Holy Spirit, in the sensation of grace. It is this revelation through sensation, which purges the soul and sets it on fire with love.

The distinction which Hilton makes between love and charity is the distinction between human and divine love. The reception of grace places the soul in a state of charity. When a person does charitable works, it is charity because it is done for God's sake alone. Hilton is careful to emphasise that Christians should not be too concerned to analyse the motivation for their good works; they speak for themselves. Unselfconscious goodness is the hallmark of the contemplatives' relation with their neighbours. 'Love', on the other hand, is no more than well-intentioned desire; human rather than divine in origin.

Hilton's spiritual teaching is aimed at restoring the relationship with God for which humankind was created. The approach to contemplation is by way of purification so that the soul may experience in this life some knowledge of the joy which should be its eternal destiny. The process of purification is paralleled by a growth in the experience of God's love through his grace; it is a benevolent view of the penitential discipline. The experience of God's love and grace is the central theme of his teaching. It is based on the idea of God as compassionate and benign rather than stern and avenging. St Augustine's vision of God was balanced; God the Father is the just judge, God the Son is long-suffering and compassionate. Hilton's emphasis seems to swing more to God as compassionate, caring and loving. It is the loss of God which is to be feared; his withdrawal is the soul's experience of the darkness of the image of sin. Yet even this is a 'lightsome darkness' to those who are reformed in faith.

Hilton's teaching illustrates the accumulative nature of the Christian tradition of the contemplative life. The notion, which Joy Russell-Smith has suggested, that Hilton is the 'creative eclectic' seems to go too far.[112] As Professor Hussey suggests this view does not sufficiently take account of the contribution of Hilton's own insights to the illumination of doctrine which is what is meant by saying the

---

[112] Russell-Smith, 'Walter Hilton', 193.

Christian tradition is accumulative. His teaching reflects the influence of Augustine's themes and the works of Gregory, Bernard, Anselm, Richard of St Victor and William Flete, to mention only well sign-posted sources, but it is also interwoven with reflections that provide a traditional, but distinctive account of the contemplative process.[113] His skilful blending of devotion for the humanity of Jesus with the notions of 'reformation in faith' and 'reformation in faith and feeling', give his teaching a personal stamp; one which gives his appropriation of the Augustinian themes a Christo-centric focus. It is a focus which also seems to meet the inchoate aspirations of fellow Christians in his life-time and indeed that make him, arguably, the most influential of the Middle English mystics.[114]

---

[113] Hussey, 'Walter Hilton: Traditionalist', 8.

[114] T.W. Coleman. *English mystics of the fourteenth century*, London: Epsworth Press, 1938, 106. Excellent as the *Scale* is, however, we may feel a little surprise that for so long it should have taken precedence over other classics of the devout life. It has not the quaint candour and picturesque homeliness of the 'Ancrene Riwle'; it lacks the poetic imagery and spiritual rapture of Richard Rolle; it has not the intellectual force and sparkling humour of the 'Cloud'; it does not share the strange touch of genius we find in Julian; nor for the variety of interest and vividness of characterisation can it compete with the 'Book of Margery Kempe'. Yet in spite of these facts it is true to say no other mystical work in our tongue has had a deeper or more abiding influence than this.

EPILOGUE

'Augustinianism' displays features of both culture and cult. It is like culture in the sense that Clifford Geertz has defined it; 'an historically transmitted pattern of meanings embodied in symbols, a system of inherited conceptions expressed in symbolic forms by means of which men communicate, perpetuate and develop their knowledge about and attitudes towards life'.[1] It is like a cult in the sense that Augustine is a witness, one whose experience gives credence to the meanings embodied in the culture. As culture it gives meaning to Christianity, offering a rationale for human life and for the world. As a cult it offers a method of practising how to live in such a world. It is open to new meaning and new method, as Augustine himself was, as the world and humankind changes.

In the foregoing discussion of particular cases we may recognise both continuity and change. Continuity in the sense that 'Augustinianism' remains recognisable as a search for the unchangeable God; change in that communities and human beings perceive themselves to be different from period to period and from each other in their needs. The process which mediates continuity and change in 'Augustinianism' we have referred to as 'transvaluation'. It embodies the characteristics of, on the one hand, transmission in the modes of receiving and interpreting and, on the other, of judgement in the sense of evaluation as counterpoint to experience and appropriation.

'Augustinianism' gained momentum as both culture and cult from the processes of Augustine's moral and intellectual conversions. The conversion processes were interactive, but the step of faith preceded understanding. With the other masters of this study it was the same; the step of faith in their cases was independent of Augustine but once it had been taken, they found in Augustine's experience a means of understanding their own. Augustine's personal experience of the grace of a loving and caring divinity was augmented by the experience of the other masters. But as the distanciation processes made Augustine's experience more remote, it tended to become a part of the cultural, rather than a cultic, experience. The universal tended to become distilled from the context of the specific experience.

---

[1]   Clifford Geertz, *The interpretation of cultures*, New York: Basic, 1973, 89.

The importance of Augustine's philosophic transvaluation of the 'affectivity' of the Judaeo-Christian inheritance lies in the cultural sphere. The 'affectivity' as the 'gracious' love of God is of ultimate importance, but the significance of the Christian worldview explained in counterpoint with the prevailing Platonic culture provided a form of continuity which anchored the personal experiences of divine 'affectivity' which were shaped by individual personalities and circumstances. It enabled individuals to appropriate the Trinitarian nature of the Christian God and the manner of its manifestation within them.

A key feature of the worldview Augustine derived from the synthesis of Hellenic and Christian insights was that of the Christian 'ascent to God' transvaluing that of the Neo-Platonic 'return to the One'. It gave meaning to the contemplative life as both 'ascent' and the inspiration for 'descent' into the active life. Moreover it gave credence to monastic existence as a transforming process, primarily contemplative, but active in the fruits it produced in the realm of evangelisation mediated by study and teaching, a counterpoint which led to the evolution of other forms of religious life.

Gregory the Great appropriated the Augustinian idea of a counterpoint between the contemplative and active lives. In the process he transvalued the Augustinian experience of divine love. He faced the pastoral challenge of a disintegrating society as Roman secular authority collapsed under the pressure of barbarian incursions. The Christian existence was not one that should be apart from the world but should be a dialectic of love drawing its power from beyond the world and sharing it abroad within the world. Gregory's success in embedding the Christian Church as the cornerstone of society was important independently of Augustine's teaching but it provided a new focus for the Augustinian worldview.

With William of St Thierry we encounter a retrieval of the contemplative influence of Augustine in a situation in which the dominant Benedictine tradition of monastic life had lost some of its original inspiration and zeal. The Cistercian reform was in some respects a return to simplicity and also to the realisation that the Christian realm was spiritual and not of this world. It was a logical extension of the Augustinian notion of conversion coupled with his Trinitarian teaching which permeated Cistercian mysticism extended and characterised by the concepts of *unitas spiritus* and *amor intellectus est.*

In the final case study of Walter Hilton there is a merging of the Augustinian insights about Christian love which emphasise both Gregory's pastoral interpretation and that of William of St Thierry's contemplative mysticism. In this case however there is also a retrieval of Augustinian and Cistercian emphases on Christ as the 'mediator' who initiates the 'ascent to God' in a process of personal 'reformation' actualised in loving care of one's neighbour. This is not the intellectualism of an Augustinian worldview but a Christo-centric application of it in the world. Walter Hilton as an Augustinian canon reflects the counterpoint in Augustine's and Gregory's lives between life in the world but not of it.

To this day Augustine of Hippo remains a symbol of a particular transvaluation of Christian teaching. His symbolic significance tends to be less cultic and more cultural. In its turn, 'Augustinianism' has been incorporated in the Aristotelian transvaluation of Christian self-understanding by St Thomas Aquinas in which Augustine's notion of human 'nature' is transformed from 'fallen' to 'unripened'. Nevertheless 'Augustinianism' has a certain autonomous significance in a spirituality that reflects the Christian understanding of the complementarity of Platonic and Aristotelian insights about a creator whose nature as one 'that is' both within and outside his creation; 'One' who leads 'above' and whose presence is apprehended through the gift of an 'anagogic' mode of the imagination.

As the product of many Christian experiences 'Augustinianism' is polysemous in character. But it is polysemous in a focussed way. It testifies to the wonder with which Augustine of Hippo reflected upon and enjoyed the boundless love of God. Some words of John Burnaby perhaps encapsulate this focus:

> The superiority of his understanding of Christianity lies in the sureness of his conviction, first that 'cleaving to God' must be the personal union of love and second, that this union is neither cause nor effect of a transformation of man's (sic) nature, but is itself that transformation (…) Augustine taught the Church that she is 'really' one with Christ only in the measure in which she 'realises' the love which is shed abroad in our hearts through the Holy Spirit which is given to us.[2]

---

[2] John Burnaby, *Amor Dei*, 179.

SELECT BIBLIOGRAPHY

Primary Sources

St Augustine:

A chronological listing of Augustine's works is available in Serge Lancel's *St Augustine*, London: SCM Press, 2002, 533-536. Latin sources are shown there in *Corpus scriptorum ecciesiasticorum latinorum*, Vienna, 1866ff.; *Patrologia cursus completus, series latina* (ed. J.P. Migne), Vols. 32-47, Paris, 1844-1864; *Corpus Christianorum*, Brepols: Turnhout, 1955 ff.; and *Bibliothèque augustinienne*, Paris: Institut d'Études Augustiniennes, 1940ff.

The following translations have been used:
Confessions (trans. E.B. Pusey), London: Dent, 1953.
The City of God (trans. J. Healey), London: Dent, 1950.
Augustine: Earlier writings (Ed. J.H.S. Burleigh), Philadelphia: Westminster Press, 1953, contains:
    Soliloquia
    De magistro
    De libero arbitrio
    De vera religione
    De utilitate credendi
    De fide et symbolo
    De diversis questionibus
Augustine: Later works (Ed. John Burnaby), Philadelphia: Westminster Press, 1955, contains:
    The Trinity, Books VIII-XV
    The Spirit and the Letter
    The Homilies on the First Epistle General of St John
Expositions on the Book of Psalms, ed. P. Schaff, (from the six volumes of the Oxford translation by A. Cleveland Coxe), Nicene and Post-Nicene Fathers, Series I, Vol. VIII, Edinburgh: T. & T. Clark, 1888.
The Rule of St Augustine (trans. Raymond C. Canning), London: Darton, Longman & Todd, 1984.

Where authors referred to in the text have used alternative translations these are referred to in footnotes.

St Bernard:

Sancti Bernardi opera (ed. J. Leclerq, C.H. Talbot, & H.M. Rochais), Vols. 1-3, Rome, 1957, 1958, 1963.

De diligendo Deo, trans. as *On the love of God* by Religious of the Community of St Mary the Virgin, London and Oxford: Mowbray, 1950.

Gregory the Great:

Homiliae in Hiezechilem Prophetam (Corpus Christianorum, series latina, cxlii, 1971), referred to as *Homilies on Ezekiel.*

Moralia in Job (Corpus Christianorum, series latina, Libri i-x, cxliii (undated), Libri xi-xxii, 1979. Libri xxiii-xxxv, 1985), referred to as *Morals* or *Morals on Job.*

Liber regulae pastoralis, PL. 77, trans. as *Pastoral care* by H.S. Bramley, London: Parker & Co., 1874.

The dialogues, ed. Mittermüller, 1880.

Walter Hilton:

Ladder of perfection, (trans. L. Sherley-Price), Harmondsworth: Penguin Books, 1957.

Scale of perfection, (ed. & introd. Evelyn Underhill), London: Watkins, 1948.

The scale of perfection, (trans., introd. & notes John P.H.Clark & Rosemary Dow-nard) Mahwah, New Jersey: Paulist Press, 1991.

Minor works of Walter Hilton, (ed. D. Jones) London: Burns, Oates & Wash-bourne, 1929; includes: *Mixed life*, Commentaries on Psalms *Qui habitat*, *Bonum est* and *Benedictus.*

Eight chapters on perfection and angels song, (trans. Rosemary Dorward) Fairacres, Oxford: S.L.G. Press, 1983.

Walter Hilton's Latin writings, (ed. J.P.H. Clark & C. Taylor) 2 Vols., Salzburg: Institut für Anglistik und Amerikanistik, 1987.

The goad of love: An unpublished translation of Walter Hilton of the Stimulus Amoris formerly attributed to St Bonaventura, (ed. C. Kirchberger) London: Faber & Faber, 1952.

Epistola de imagine peccati, Br. Lib. MS Royal 6. E III f.72-76.

Epistola de utilitate et prerogativis religionis, Bodleian Lib., MS. Lat. Theolog. e.26.f. 120-138 (addressed to Adam Horsley).

Epistola ad quondam seculo renunciare volentem, Br.Lib.,MS Royal 6 E III, f.113-120.

Epistola ad quemdam solitarium de leccione, intercione, oracione, meditatione, etc. Br.Lib., MS Royal 6 E III f.120-122

Tractatus de adoracione imaginum (against Wycliffe), Br.Lib., MS Royal II Bx 1.178-183.

Mabillon, J. *Annales ordinis S Benedicti occidentalium monachorum patriarchae* (to AD 1066; 4 vols.), Lutetiae-Parisiorum: Sumtibus Caroli Robustel, 1703-1707.

Pascal, B. *Pensées*, (ed. L. Brunschvicg) Paris: Cluny, 1934.

Plotinus, *Enneads*, (trans. Stephen McKenna; 4th ed. revised, by B.S. Page) London: Faber & Faber, 1969.

St Possidius, 'Life of St Augustine', in: F.R. Hoare (Ed.), *The Western fathers*, London: Sheed and Ward, 1954, 191-244.

Rupert of Deutz, *De Trinitate* (PL.167).

William of St Thierry:

De contemplando Deo, (PL.184: 365-380). Tranlated as *On contemplating God, prayer,* [*Oratio*], *meditations,* [*Meditativae orationes*, PL.180: 205-248] (*The works of William of St. Thierry*, Vol.1; trans. Sr. Penelope [Lawson]), Spencer, MA: Cistercian Publications, 1971.

De natura et dignitate amoris (PL.184: 379-408). Translated as *The nature and dignity of love,* (trans. T.X. Davis, introd. & notes David N. Bell) Kalamazoo, MI: Cistercian Publications, 1981

Oratio, trans. as cited above, *The works of William of St Thierry*, Vol. 1.

Meditativae orationes, trans. as cited above, *The works of William of St Thierry*, Vol. 1.

Expositio super Cantica canticorum, (PL.18O: 475-546). Translated as *Exposition on the Song of Songs* (*The works of William of St.Thierry*, Vol. 2; trans. Sr Columba Hart), Spencer, MA: Cistercian Publications, 1970.

Speculum fidei and *Aenigma fidei*, (PL.180: 365-398; 397-440). Translations:
    The mirror of faith, (trans. T.X. Davis) Kalamazoo, MI: Cistercian Publications, 1974.
    The enigma of faith, (trans. J.D. Anderson) Kalamazoo, MI: Cistercian Publications, 1974.

Epistola ad Fratres de Mont-Dei (*Epistola Aurea*) (PL.184: 307-354). Translated as: *The golden epistle: A letter to the Brethren at Mont Dieu,* (*The works of William of St Thierry*, Vol.4; trans. T. Berkeley) Spencer, MA: Cistercian Publications, 1971.

De sacramento altaris (PL.180: 341-366)

De natura corporis et animae (PL.180: 695-726). Translated as: *The nature of the body and soul,* (trans. B. Clark), in: B. McGinn (ed.), *Three treatises on man:*

A Cistercian anthropology, Kalamazoo, MI: Cistercian Publications, 1977, 101-152.
Super Cantica canticorum ex operibus Sancti Ambrosii (PL.15: 1849-1885).
Super Cantica canticorum ex operibus Sancti Gregorii (PL.180: 441-474).
Disputatio adversus Petrum Abelardum (PL.180: 249-282).
De erroribus Guillelmi de Conches (PL.180: 333-340).
Expositio in Epistolam ad Romanos (PL.180: 547-694). Translation: *Exposition on the Epistle to the Romans,* (trans. J.B. Hasbrouck) Kalamazoo, MI: Cistercian Publications, 1980.
Brevis commentatio in priora duo capita cantici canticorum (PL.184: 407-436).
Vita Bernardi (PL.185: 225-268).

Secondary Literature

Adam, A., *Guillaume de Saint-Thierry. Sa vie et ses oeuvres,* Bourg-en-Bresse, 1923.
Baldwin, A.P., 'The tripartite reformation of the soul in "The Scale of Perfection", "Pearl" and "Piers Plowman"', in: M. Glasscoe (Ed.), *The mediaeval mystical tradition in England.* Papers read at Dartington Hall, July 1984, Exeter: University of Exeter, 1984, 136-149.
Bell, D.N., *The image and likeness: The Augustinian spirituality of William of St Thierry,* Kalamazoo: Cistercian Publications, 1984.
Berlière, U., 'Les origines de Citeaux et l'ordre Benedictin au XIIe siècle', in: *Revue d'Histoire Ecclesiastique* 1 (1900), 448-471 and 2 (1901), 253-290.
Bouyer, L., *La spiritualité de Citeaux,* Paris: Portulan, 1954. (Trans. E.A. Livingstone as *The Cistercian heritage,* Westminster, MD: Newman Press, 1958.)
Bouyer, L., *A history of Christian spirituality* (trans. Mary R. Ryan). Vol.1: *The spirituality of the New Testament fathers,* London: Burns & Oates, 1968, reprinted 1982.
Brooke, C.N., *The twelfth century renaissance,* London: Thames & Hudson, 1969.
Brooke, O., *Studies in monastic theology,* Kalamazoo: Cistercian Publications, 1980 (Cistercian Studies Series 37).
Brown, P., *Augustine of Hippo: A biography,* London: Faber & Faber, 1967.
Brown, P., *The world of late antiquity,* London: Thames & Hudson, 1971.
Brown, P., *Religion and society in the age of St Augustine,* London: Faber & Faber, 1973.
Brown, P., *Cult of the saints: Its rise and function in Latin Christianity,* London: S.C.M. Press, 1981.

Burnaby, J., *Amor Dei: A study of the religion of St Augustine,* London: Hodder & Stoughton, 1938.

Butler, C., *Western mysticism: The teaching of Augustine, Gregory and Bernard on contemplation and the contemplative life,* London: Constable, 1967.

Cayré, F., *La contemplation Augustienne: Principes de la spiritualité de S. Augustin,* Paris: Blot, 1927.

Ceglar, S., 'William of St Thierry: The chronology of his life with study of his treatise *On the Nature of Love,* his authorship of the *Brevis Commentatio,* the *In Lacu* and the *Reply to Cardinal Mathew*', Ann Arbor: University Micro-films, 1971.

Chadwick, H., *The early Church,* Harmondsworth: Penguin Books, 1967.

Chadwick, H., *Augustine,* Oxford: Oxford University Press, 1986.

Clark, J.P.H., 'The lightsome darkness: Aspects of Walter Hilton's theological background', in: *Downside Review* 95 (1977), 95-109.

Clark, J.P.H., 'The "Cloud of Unknowing" – Walter Hilton and St John of the Cross: A comparison', in: *Downside Review* 96 (1978), 281-298.

Clark, J.P.H., 'Walter Hilton and "Liberty of Spirit"', in: *Downside Review* 96 (1978), 61-78.

Clark, J.P.H., 'Action and contemplation in Walter Hilton', in: *Downside Review* 97 (1979), 258-274.

Clark, J.P.H., 'Image and likeness in Walter Hilton', in: *Downside Review* 97 (1979), 204-220.

Clark, J.P.H., 'Intention in Walter Hilton', in: *Downside Review* 97 (1979), 69-80.

Clark, J.P.H., 'Augustine, Anselm and Walter Hilton', in: Marion Glasscoe (Ed.), *Mediaeval mystical tradition in England.* Papers read at Dartington Hall, July 1982, Exeter: University of Exeter, 1982, 102-126.

Coleman, T.W., *English mystics of the fourteenth century,* London: Epsworth Press, 1938.

Colledge, E., *The mediaeval mystics of England,* London: Murray, 1962.

Copleston, F., *Augustine to Bonaventure (A history of philosophy,* Vol.2, Part 1), New York: Image Books, 1962.

Copleston, F., *Ockham to the speculative mystics (A history of philosophy,* Vol.3, Part 1), New York: Image Books, 1963.

Cross, F.L. (Ed.), *Oxford dictionary of the Christian church,* Oxford: Oxford University Press, Second edition, 1974; reprinted 1984.

Daniélou, J., *Platonisme et théologie mystique,* Paris: Montaigne, 1944.

Deanesly, M., *A history of the mediaeval church, 590-1500,* London: Methuen, 8th ed., 1954. (orig. publ. 1925)

Déchanet, J.M., 'Les maîtres et les modèles: Guillaume de St Thierry', in: *La Vie Spirituelle* 53 (1937), 40-64.

Déchanet, J.M., 'A propos de la Lettre aux Frères du Mont-Dieu', in: *Collectanea Ordinis Cisterciensium Reformatorum* 5 (1938), 3-8, 81-95.

Déchanet, J.M., *William of St Thierry: The man and his work,* (trans., Richard Strachan) Spencer, MA.: Cistercian Publications, 1972 (Cistercian Studies Series 10).

Dickinson, J.C., *The origin of the Austin canons and their introduction into England,* London: SPCK, 1950.

Diehl, P.S., *The mediaeval European religious lyric: An "ars poetica",* Berkeley: University of California Press, 1985.

Dudden, F.H., *Gregory the Great: His place in history and thought,* London: Longman, Green, and Co., 1905, 2 vols.

Durkheim, E., 'The social foundations of religion', in: R. Robertson (Ed.), *Sociology of religion,* Harmondsworth: Penguin Books, 1969, 42-54.

Emden, A.B., *Biographical register of the University of Cambridge to 1500,* Cambridge: Cambridge University Press, 1963.

Evans, G.R., *The thought of Gregory the Great,* Cambridge: Cambridge University Press, 1986.

Gardner, H.L., 'Walter Hilton and the authorship of "The Cloud of Unknowing"', in: *Review of English Studies* 9 (1933), 129-147.

Gardner, H.L., 'The text of the Scale of Perfection', in: *Medium Aevum* 5 (1936), 11-30.

Gardner, H.L., 'Walter Hilton and the mystical tradition in England', in: *Essays and Studies* 22 (1937), 103-127.

Geertz, C., 'Religion as a cultural system', in: idem, *The interpretation of cultures,* London: Hutchinson, 1975.

Gilson, E., *La philosophie au Moyen Age,* Paris: Payot, 1930.

Gilson, E., *Héloise et Abelard,* Paris: Vrin, 1938.

Gilson, E., *The spirit of mediaeval philosophy,* (trans. A.H.C. Downes) New York: Charles Scribner's Sons, 1940. (orig. publ. 1932)

Gilson, E., *The mystical theology of St Bernard,* (trans. A.H.C. Downes) New York: Sheed & Ward, 1955 (orig. publ. 1934).

Gilson, E., *The Christian philosophy of Saint Augustine,* (trans. L.E.M. Lynch) London: Gollancz, 1960 (orig. publ. 1929).

Green, J.D., *A strange tongue,* Leuven: Peeters, 2002.

Green, V.V.H., *The later Plantagenets,* London: Edward & Arnold, 1953.

Gregorovius, F., *History of the city of Rome in the Middle Ages,* (trans. G.W. Hamilton & A. Hamilton) 13 Vols., London: Bell, 1895-1902.

Happold, F.C., *Mysticism,* Harmondsworth: Penguin books, 1963.

Harnack, A., *History of dogma,* 3rd ed., 7 Vols., London: Williams & Norgate, 1896-99; and New York: Russell & Russell, 1958.

Haskins, C.H., *The renaissance of the twelfth century,* Cambridge, MA: Harvard University Press, 1939 (first published 1927).

Heath, Peter, *Church and realm 1272-1461,* London: Fontana Press, 1988.

Heer, F., *The mediaeval world,* (trans. J. Sandheimer) London: Weidenfeld & Nicholson, 1962. (orig. publ. 1961)

Henry, P., *La vision d'Ostie,* Paris: Vrin, 1938.

Hick, J., *Evil and the God of love,* London: Collins, 1974.

Hodgson, P., *Cloud of Unknowing and related treatises,* Salzburg: Institut Fur Anglistik und Amerikanistik, 1982.

Holmes, U.T., *A history of Christian spirituality: An analytical introduction,* New York: Seabury Press, 1980.

Hussey, S.S., 'Walter Hilton, traditionalist', in: M. Glasscoe (Ed.), *Mediaeval mystical tradition in England.* Papers read at the Exeter Symposium, July 1980, Exeter: University of Exeter, 1980, 1-16.

Inge, W.R., *Christian mysticism,* London: Methuen & Co Ltd, 1899.

Javelet, R., *Image et resemblance au XIIe siècle: De Saint Anselme a Alain de Lille,* Paris: Letouzey et Ané, 1967.

Kieckhefer, R., *Unquiet souls: Fourteenth century saints and their religious milieu,* Chicago: University of Chicago Press, 1984.

Knowles, D., & Hadcock, R.N., *Mediaeval religious houses, England and Wales,* London: Longmans, 1953.

Knowles, M.D., *The English mystical tradition,* London: Burns and Oates, 1961.

Ladner, G.B., *The idea of reform: Its impact on Christian thought and action in the age of the Fathers,* Cambridge MA.: Harvard University Press, 1959.

Lancel, S., *St Augustine,* London: SCM Press, 2002.

Lawrence, C.M., *Mediaeval monasticism, Forms of religious life in Western Europe in the Middle Ages,* London-New York: Longman, 1984.

Leclerq, J., Vandenbroucke, F., & Bouyer, L., *The spirituality of the Middle Ages,* New York: Seabury Press, 1982.

Lonergan, B., *Method in theology,* London: Darton, Longman & Todd, 1972; reprinted second ed., 1975.

Louth, A., *The origins of the Christian mystical tradition from Plato to Dionysius,* Oxford: Oxford University Press, 1985.

Luscombe, D.E., *The school of Peter Abelard: The influence of Abelard's thought in the early scholastic period,* Cambridge: Cambridge University Press, 1969.

Malévez, L., 'La doctrine de l'image et de la connaissance mystique chez Guillaume de St Thierry', in: *Recherches de Science Religieuse* 22 (1932), 178-205; 257-279.

Markus, R.A., '"Imago" and "Similitudo" in Augustine', in: *Revue des Études Augustiniennes* 10 (1964), 125-143.

Markus, R.A., *Christianity in the Roman world,* London: Thames & Hudson, 1974.

Markus, R.A., *Gregory the Great and his world,* Cambridge: Cambridge University Press, 1997.

McGinn, B., *The Growth of Mysticism* (Vol.I of *The Presence of God: A History of Western Christian Mysticism*), New York: Crossroad, 1994.

McFarlane, K.B., *John Wycliffe and the beginnings of English non-conformity,* London: English Universities Press, 1952.

Monceaux, P., *Histoire de la littérature Latine Chrétienne,* Paris: Payot, 1924.

O'Donnell, J.B., *Augustine: Saint & sinner,* London: Profile Books, 2005.

Panofsky, E., *Renaissance and renascences in Western art,* London: Paladin Books, 1970.

Pantin, W.A., *The English Church in the fourteenth century,* Cambridge: Cambridge University Press, 1955.

Pelikan, J., *The emergence of the Catholic tradition (100-600) (The Christian tradition: A history of the development of doctrine.* Vol.1), Chicago-London: University of Chicago Press, 1971.

Pelikan, J., *The growth of mediaeval theology (600-1300) (The Christian tradition: A history of the development of doctrine.* Vol.3), Chicago-London: University of Chicago Press, 1978.

Pelikan, J., *Reformation of Church and Dogma (1300-1700) (The Christian tradition: A history of the development of doctrine.* Vol.4), Chicago-London: University of Chicago Press, 1984.

Petersen, J.M., *The Dialogues of Gregory the Great in their late antique cultural background,* Toronto: Pontifical Institute of Mediaeval Studies, 1984 (Studies and Texts 69).

Poncelet, A. (Ed.), 'Vie ancienne de Guillaume de Saint-Thierry' in: *Mélanges Godefroid Kurth.* Vol. 1, Liège: Université de Liège, Faculté de Philosophie et Lettres, 1908, 85-96.

Portalié, E., *A guide to the thought of St Augustine,* (trans. A.J. Bastian) Chicago: H. Regenery Co, 1960 (orig. publ. 1902).

Pourrat, P., *Christian spirituality* (4. vols), Westminster, Md: Newman Press, 1953-1955 (orig. publ. 1918)

Powicke, F.M., *Christian life in the Middle Ages,* Oxford: Clarendon Press, 1935.

Riehle, W., *The middle English mystics,* (trans. Bernard Strandring) London: Routledge & Kegan Paul, 1981. (orig. publ. 1977)

Rousselot, P., *Pour l'histoire du problème de l'amour au Moyen Age,* Münster: Aschendorffsche Buchhandlung, 1933 (reimpr. of the doctoral dissertation Paris, 1907).

Russell-Smith, J., 'In defense of the veneration of images', in: *Dominican Studies* 7 (1954), 180-214.

Russell-Smith, J., 'Walter Hilton', in: J. Walsh (Ed.), *Pre-reformation English spirituality*, New York: Fordham University Press, 1965, 182-197.

Sargent, M.G., 'A new manuscript of "The Chastising of God's Children" with an ascription to Walter Hilton', in: *Medium Aevum* 46 (1977), 49-65.

Sargent, M.G., 'The organisation of the Scale of Perfection', in: M. Glasscoe (Ed.), *Mediaeval mystical tradition in England*. Papers read at Dartington Hall, July 1982, Exeter: University of Exeter, 1982, 231-261.

Sitwell, G., 'Walter Hilton', in: *The Clergy Review* 44 (1959), 321-332.

Smalley, B., *The study of the Bible in the Middle Ages*, Oxford: Blackwell, 1952.

Southern, R.W., *The making of the Middle Ages*, London: Hutchinson's University Library, 1953.

Southern, R.W., *Western society and the church in the Middle Ages*, Harmondsworth: Penguin Books, 1970.

Stormon E.J., 'The spirituality of St Augustine', 'The Spirituality of St Bernard' and 'The English Mystics', in: N.J. Ryan (Ed.), *Christian spiritual theology*, Melbourne: Dove Communications Pty Ltd., 1976, 129-172.

Sullivan, J.E., *The image of God: The doctrine of St Augustine and its influence*, Dubuque, Ia: Priory Press, 1963.

Taylor, H.O., *The mediaeval mind: A history of the developments of thought and emotion in the Middle Ages*, London: Macmillan and Co. Ltd., 1911.

Thornton, M., *English spirituality: An outline of ascetical theology according to the English pastoral tradition*, Cambridge, MA.: Cowley 1986.

Thurston, H., *The physical phenomenon of mysticism*, London: Burns Oates, 1952.

Tracy, D., *The analogical imagination*, New York: Crossroad, 1991.

Ullmann, W., *Mediaeval foundations of renaissance humanism*, London: Elek, 1977.

Underhill, E., *Mysticism: A study in the nature and developments of man's spiritual consciousness*, London: Methuen, 1949.

Underhill, E., *The mystics of the Church*, London: James Clarke, 1925.

Van der Meer, F., *Augustine the Bishop: The life and work of a father of the Church*, (trans. E. Battershaw & G.R. Lamb) London: Sheed & Ward, 1978 (orig. publ. 1947).

Williams, Rowan, *Wound of knowledge*, London: Darton, Longman & Todd, 1981.

Wills, G., *Saint Augustine*, London: Penguin Books, 2005.

Wilmart, A., 'La serie et la date des ouvrages de Guillaume de Saint Thierry', in: *Revue Mabillon* 14 (1924), 156-167.

Windelband, W., *Geschichte der Philosophie*, Tübingen, 1910. (Eng. trans. *A history of philosophy*, New York: Harper, 1958).

PRINTED ON PERMANENT PAPER • IMPRIME SUR PAPIER PERMANENT • GEDRUKT OP DUURZAAM PAPIER - ISO 9706

N.V. PEETERS S.A., WAROTSTRAAT 50, B-3020 HERENT